AQA Religious Studies B

Religious Expression in Society

GCSE

Marianne Fleming

Anne Jordan

Peter Smith

David Worden

Series editor

Cynthia Bartlett

Nelson Thornes

15\01

Published in 2009 by:
Nelson Thornes Ltd
Delta Place
27 Bath Road
CHELTENHAM
GL53 7TH
United Kingdom

09 10 11 12 13 / 10 9 8 7 6 5 4 3 2 1

A catalogue record for this book is available from the British Library

ISBN 978 1 4085 0516 8

Cover photograph/illustration by Corbis/ Pascal Deloche/ Godong

Illustrations by Pantek Arts Ltd, Paul McCaffrey (c/o Sylvie Poggio Agency) and Rupert Besley

Page make-up by Pantek Arts Ltd, Maidstone

Printed and bound in Spain by GraphyCems

Photo Acknowledgements

iStockphoto: 1.2A, 1.2B, 1.3A, 1.3B, 1.4A, 1.6A, 1.6C, 1.7A, 1.7B, 1.9C, 1.9D, 1.10C, 1.10D, 1.11A, 2.1C, 2.1E, 2.2A, 2.2B, 2.4A, 2.5A, 2.5B, 2.7B, 2.8A, 2.8C, 2.9A, 2.10B, 3.1B 3.1C, 3.2B, 3.3A, 3.3B, 3.4A, 3.4B, 3.5C, 3.7B, 3.10B, 3.11A, 4.1A(header), 4.1B, 4.1C, 4.4B, 4.7A, 4.8A, 4.8B, 4.9B, 5.1A, 5.3A, 5.4A, 5.5C, 5.10A, 5.10C, 6.1B, 6.3B, 6.5B, 6.8A(header), 6.8C, 6.9A, 6.9C, 6.10A, 6.10C **Fotolia:** 1.1A, 1.1C, 1.3C, 1.4B, 1.4C, 1.6B, 1.8A, 1.9A, 1.10A, 1.10B, Chapter Two (header), 2.1A, 2.1B, 2.1F, 2.2C, 2.3A, 2.3B, 2.4C, 2.5C, 2.5D, 2.9C, 2.11A, 3.1A, 3.4C, 3.4D, 3.5B, 3.8A, 3.8B, 3.9A, 4.6B, 4.7C, 4.10A, 4.10B,.4.11A, 5.1B, 5.6A, 5.7A, 5.7B, 5.7C, 5.9A, 5.10B, 5.11A, 6.2A, 6.2B, 6.5A, 6.6A, 6.7B, 6.11A **Peter Smith:** 6.3A, 6.4A, 6.4B, 6.7A, 6.7C, **Anne Jordan:** 2.2C, 2.6A, 2.6B, 2.9B **Alamy**; Rolf Richardson 2.6C, Alexei Fateev, 2.7A, Tibor Bognar 2.10A, Paul Doyle 2.10B, 3.3C Kevin Galvin / Alamy. Mirrorpix 4.1C, Helene Rogers 4.5B, image100 4.6A, Charles Stirling (Travel) 5.5B, Denis Kennedy 6.1A, **Getty:** 3.6A, 5.3B, 5.6B, Time & Life Pictures 3.5A, AFP, 4.5A, 6.8B, 5.5A, 6.8B **Rex features:** 1.1B, 5.2A, 5.2B, 5.8A, 5.9B, 6.10B, **PA photos:** 4.2B, 5.4B, 5.8B, 6.6D **Ark Religion.com:** 1.3D, 2.7C, 3.7A, 3.10A **Ann & Bury Peerless Picture Library:** 1.9B **Colin Sutton:** 2.1D **BBC Photo Library:** 4.3A, 4.3B **Walt Disney Pictures/Walden Media/The Kobal Collection:** 3.2A **Tate, London 2009:** 1.5A, **NI Syndication:** 4.4A **www.bbfc.co.uk;** The symbols are the property of the British Board of Film Classification and are trademark and copyright protected 4.7B

Text Acknowledgements

Scripture quotations taken from the Holy Bible, New International Version. Copyright © 1978, 1984 by International Bible Society. Used by permission of Hodder & Stoughton, a division of Hodder Headline Ltd. All rights reserved. "NIV" is a registered trademark of International Bible Society. UK trademark number 1448790.

3.2, 1.9, Extracts from *THE HOLY QURAN TRANSLATION AND COMMENTARY* by Abdullah Yusuf Ali. Reprinted with permission of IPCI – 1.4 page 15 Short quote by Antony Gormley about The Angel of the North, from www.gateshead.gov.uk. Reprinted with permission of the author, 1.5 page 16 The English Translation of The Apostle's Creed by the International Consultation on English Texts ICET, 3.1 page 52 Short quote from 'The Fringe Benefits of Failure and the Importance of Imagination' J. K. Rowling, Harvard Commencement Speech June, 2008. Reprinted with permisison of Harvard University, 3.2B 'A doctor, a lawyer…' submitted by L. M. Myers to www.inspirationalarchivc.com, 3.6 page 63 extract from 'The Diary of a Church Mouse' by John Betjeman, from COLLECTED POEMS © 1955, 1958, 1962, 1964, 1968, 1970, 1979, 1981, 1982, 2001, published by John Murray. Reprinted with permission of John Murray Publishers

Contents

Introduction   5

1   Religion and art   8

1.1   The nature of spirituality   8

1.2   What is religious art?   10

1.3   Icons, paintings and stained glass   12

1.4   Calligraphy, graffiti and sculpture   14

1.5   The Resurrection in Cookham
Churchyard – a case study   16

1.6   How and why religions use art   18

1.7   How religious art is used in worship   20

1.8   The impact of religious art   22

1.9   What does religious art tell us
about God, belief and the artist?   24

1.10   The symbolic nature of religious art
and its place in the modern world   26

Chapter 1: Assessment guidance   28

2   Religion and architecture   30

2.1   What is architecture?   30

2.2   What is religious architecture?   32

2.3   The production of religious
architecture   34

2.4   Architecture for public places of
worship   36

2.5   Graveyards, statues and monuments 38

2.6   St Michael's Cathedral, Coventry –
a case study   40

2.7   How religious architecture is used
in worship   42

2.8   The impact of religious architecture 44

2.9   What does religious architecture tell us
about God, belief and the architect?   46

2.10   The symbolic nature of religious
architecture and its place in the
modern world   48

Chapter 2: Assessment guidance   50

3   Religion and literature   52

3.1   What is literature?   52

3.2   What is religious literature?   54

3.3   The production of religious literature 56

3.4   Holy books and books of teachings   58

3.5   Fiction and poetry with a religious
message   60

3.6   'Diary of a Church Mouse' –
a case study   62

3.7   How religious literature is used
in worship   64

3.8   The impact of religious literature   66

3.9   What does religious literature tell us
about God, belief and the writer?   68

3.10   The symbolic nature of religious
literature and its place in the
modern world   70

Chapter 3: Assessment guidance   72

4   Religion and the media   74

4.1   What is the media?   74

4.2   How is religion portrayed on
television?   76

4.3   *The Vicar of Dibley* – a case study   78

4.4   How is religion portrayed in
newspapers and magazines?   80

4.5	The power of the press	82
4.6	Censorship and blasphemy	84
4.7	Censorship and religious influence	86
4.8	How and why do religions use the media?	88
4.9	What do religious media tell us about God, belief and media producers?	90
4.10	Spirituality and the media	92
	Chapter 4: Assessment guidance	94

5 Religion and music — **96**

5.1	Why do people listen to music?	96
5.2	Different types of music	98
5.3	Religious music	100
5.4	'Zadok the Priest' – a case study	102
5.5	How and why do religions use music?	104
5.6	The impact of religious music	106
5.7	What does religious music tell us about God, belief and composers and lyricists?	108
5.8	Cat Stevens/Yusuf Islam – a case study	110
5.9	Spirituality and music	112
5.10	The symbolic nature of music	114
	Chapter 5: Assessment guidance	116

6 Religion in contemporary society — **118**

6.1	The expression of spirituality in society	118
6.2	What does membership of a faith involve?	120
6.3	Religious communities	122
6.4	Belmont Abbey, Hereford – a case study	124
6.5	Religious symbols	126
6.6	Nadia Eweida – a case study	128
6.7	Acts of worship	130
6.8	How does worship affect individual people?	132
6.9	The impact of religion	134
6.10	Difficulties arising from expressing spirituality	136
	Chapter 6: Assessment guidance	138
	Glossary	140
	Index	142

Nelson Thornes has worked in partnership with AQA to make sure that this book offers you the best possible support for your GCSE course. All the content has been approved by the senior examining team at AQA, so you can be sure that it gives you just what you need when you are preparing for your exams.

■ How to use this book

This book covers everything you need for your course.

Learning Objectives

At the beginning of each section or topic you'll find a list of Learning Objectives based on the requirements of the specification, so you can make sure you are covering everything you need to know for the exam.

> **Objectives**
>
> **Objectives**
>
> **Objectives**
>
> **Objectives**
>
> First objective.
>
> Second objective.

AQA Examiner's Tips

Don't forget to look at the AQA Examiner's Tips throughout the book to help you with your study and prepare for your exam.

> **AQA Examiner's tip**
>
> Don't forget to look at the AQA Examiner's Tips throughout the book to help you with your study and prepare for your exam.

AQA Examination-style Questions

These offer opportunities to practise doing questions in the style that you can expect in your exam so that you can be fully prepared on the day.

AQA examination questions are reproduced by permission of the Assessment and Qualifications Alliance.

AQA GCSE Religious Expression in Society

This book is written specifically for GCSE students studying the AQA Religious Studies Specification B, *Unit 5 Religious Expression in Society*. The expressive arts are a way of expressing personal insights, ideas and emotions through art, architecture, literature, music and the media.

You do not have to be religious to study this course. You simply need to be interested in developing your knowledge, skills and understanding of religion by exploring the different ways in which the arts are used to express religious beliefs in society today.

■ Topics in this unit

In the examination you will be asked to answer four questions, based on four of the following six topics. For each topic you will need to be able to discuss a particular piece of expressive art.

Religion and art

This topic explores different types of religious art and how it is used in public and private worship. It discusses how and why such art is produced, and what it can tell us about God, belief and the artist.

Religion and architecture

This topic explores different types of religious architecture and how it is used in public and private worship. It discusses how and why such architecture is produced, and what it can tell us about God, belief and the architect.

Religion and literature

This topic explores different types of religious literature and how it is used in public and private worship. It discusses how and why such literature is produced, and what it can tell us about God, belief and the writer.

Religion and the media

This topic explores various forms of the media, the positive and negative sides of religious portrayal in it, and how and why religions use it. It discusses the impact of religious media on believers and non-believers.

Religion and music

This topic explores different types of religious music, and how it is used in public and private worship. It discusses how and why such music is produced, and what it can tell us about God, belief and the composer/lyricist.

Religion in contemporary society

This topic explores how people express their religion and spirituality in modern society, discussing positive and negative aspects of this expression.

■ Assessment guidance

The examination questions allow you to refer to the religion(s) you have studied. To encourage you to practise the type of question that will be set, each chapter in this book concludes with Assessment guidance. Each topic in the examination will include an evaluation question marked out of six marks. It will help you to write better answers yourself, if you understand what the examiners are looking for. To assist you in this, each assessment guidance spread includes an example for you to mark, using the scheme below. Make sure that you understand the differences between the standard of answer for each level, and what you need to do to achieve full marks.

Examination questions will test two assessment objectives

| AO1 | Describe, explain and analyse, using knowledge and understanding. | 50% |
| AO2 | Use evidence and reasoned argument to express and evaluate personal responses, informed insights, and differing viewpoints. | 50% |

The examiner will also take into account the quality of your written communication – how clearly you express yourself and how well you communicate your meaning. The grid below also gives you some guidance on the sort of quality examiners expect to see at different levels.

Levels of response mark scheme for six-mark evaluation questions

Levels	Criteria for AO1	Criteria for AO2	Quality of written communication	Marks
0	Nothing relevant or worthy of credit	An unsupported opinion or no relevant evaluation	The candidate's presentation, spelling, punctuation and grammar seriously obstruct understanding	0 marks
Level 1	Something relevant or worthy of credit	An opinion supported by simple reason	The candidate presents some relevant information in a simple form. The text produced is usually legible. Spelling, punctuation and grammar allow meaning to be derived, although errors are sometimes obstructive	1 mark
Level 2	Elementary knowledge and understanding, e.g. two simple points	An opinion supported by one developed reason or two simple reasons		2 marks
Level 3	Sound knowledge and understanding	An opinion supported by one well developed reason or several simple reasons. **N.B. Candidates who make no religious comment should not achieve more than Level 3**	The candidate presents relevant information in a way which assists with the communication of meaning. The text produced is legible. Spelling, punctuation and grammar are sufficiently accurate not to obscure meaning	3 marks
Level 4	A clear knowledge and understanding with some development	An opinion supported by two developed reasons with reference to religion		4 marks
Level 5	A detailed answer with some analysis, as appropriate	Evidence of reasoned consideration of two different points of view, showing informed insights and knowledge and understanding of religion	The candidate presents relevant information coherently, employing structure and style to render meaning clear. The text produced is legible. Spelling, punctuation and grammar are sufficiently accurate to render meaning clear	5 marks
Level 6	A full and coherent answer showing good analysis, as appropriate	A well-argued response, with evidence of reasoned consideration of two different points of view showing informed insights and ability to apply knowledge and understanding of religion effectively		6 marks

Note: In evaluation answers to questions worth only 3 marks, the first three levels apply. Questions that are marked out of 3 marks do not ask for two views, but simply for your opinion.

Successful study of this unit will result in a Short Course GCSE award. Study of one further unit will provide a Full Course GCSE award. Other units in Specification B that may be taken to achieve a Full Course GCSE award are:

- Unit 1 Religion and Citizenship
- Unit 2 Religion and Life Issues
- Unit 3 Religion and Morality
- Unit 4 Religious Philosophy and Ultimate Questions
- Unit 6 Worship and Key Beliefs.

1 Religion and art

1.1 The nature of spirituality

■ The search for spirituality

Many people are searching for a meaning in life. They are seeking answers to spiritual questions such as 'Why are we here?' and 'What happens when we die?' These are spiritual questions that have been answered for religious believers by the teachings of their faith. Some people who are not religious believers are also concerned with spiritual matters and seek to escape from the **materialism** of the modern world.

■ The nature of a material world

It is often said that people are less interested in **spirituality** than they used to be and that materialism dominates the modern world. When people are thinking about what designer clothes to buy or whether they must have the latest gadget, they are behaving in a material way. Materialists tend to be concerned with how they look to others, and consider that happiness comes from having the latest and best things. They think it is outward appearances that matter and do not think about spiritual matters.

■ The nature of spirituality

It is very difficult to describe spirituality. Some people reject materialism as they do not believe that it brings happiness. They believe that happiness comes from spiritual things. They seek answers to spiritual questions about life, and spirituality becomes a powerful influence in their lives. Religious people find answers to spiritual questions through the teachings of their religion. They believe that these spiritual truths provide acceptable answers but not total understanding of the meaning and purpose of life. For many, these truths extend beyond this world into the possibility of an afterlife.

What is spiritual truth?

Spiritual truth is what a believer claims to be true about the existence of God, the origin of the universe and/or the purpose of life. Believers who make claims about the truth of their religious beliefs may give as evidence: the religious authority and sacred writings that they accept; their conscience, which they might regard as the inner voice of God; religious experience; the history of the religion; scientific theories about the origin of the universe; and observation of the natural world. What believers understand to be spiritual truth may influence the art, architecture, literature, music and media produced by the individual, religious community and/or society.

> **Objectives**
>
> Understand the nature of spirituality and materialism.
>
> Explore how spirituality might be expressed.

> **Key terms**
>
> **Materialism:** belief in the importance of personal possessions.
>
> **Spirituality:** a sense of something which is not material or temporal, usually to do with religion.

∞ links

The powerful influence and place of spirituality in the modern world is discussed throughout the book.

A *Do we live in a material world?*

Discussion activity

With a partner, in a small group or as a whole class, discuss the following statement: 'It does not matter what you look like on the outside, it is what you are like on the inside that counts.' Do you agree? Give reasons for your answer, showing that you have thought about more than one point of view.

B   *Mother Teresa combined the spiritual life of a nun with helping the dying on the streets of Calcutta*

Research activity

1   Using the internet and/or a library, find out why Mother Teresa decided to become a nun and devote her life to those in need.

How is spirituality expressed?

There are so many different ways in which people feel spiritual, and in which spirituality is expressed. For some people, spirituality is expressed by taking part in an act of worship or by engaging in prayer or meditation. Some people believe that they have a spiritual calling (a vocation). This could be to leave their daily lives and become a monk or nun so that they can give themselves fully, without distractions, to a spiritual life. Others choose to express their spirituality by helping others. They may feel 'called' to become a doctor, teacher, social worker or may simply seek opportunities to help others.

Some people are inspired to express these feelings of spirituality about God or the meaning of life creatively through art, architecture, literature or music. They believe that the inspiration for their work comes from a source outside themselves. When others see, read or listen to their work, they also often feel emotions – such as joy or sadness – that may be described as spiritual. However, although an individual's response to the work may be spiritual, it may not be religious. Individuals can have spiritual experiences without accepting the teachings of a religious tradition.

There are occasions when creative work is considered by religious people to be blasphemy. For example, it would be considered blasphemous for Muslims to draw a picture of Allah or Muhammad.

C   *Some people experience spirituality by playing or listening to music*

∞ links

The topic of blasphemy is discussed in association with other topics pages 66–67 and 84–85. See the Glossary at the back of the book for a definition.

Research activity

2   Using the Internet and/or a dictionary write a definition of what a religious believer means by the term 'blasphemy'.

AQA   Examiner's tip

Make sure that you can explain the terms 'spirituality' and 'materialism', and that you understand the difference between them.

Activities

1   Explain what is meant by 'materialism' and give an example.
2   Explain what is meant by 'spirituality' and give an example.
3   Explain what is meant by 'spiritual truth'.
4   Make a list of different ways in which spirituality may be expressed. Try to think of as many as possible.

Summary

You should now be able to explain the difference between spirituality and materialism, and identify how spirituality might be expressed.

1.2 What is religious art?

◼ Defining religious art

Religious **art** tries to express a spiritual message in some way. It includes a wide variety of works of art including drawing, paintings and sculpture. Art may be called religious when it includes some of the following characteristics.

Art that contains religious themes

The purpose of the work of art that contains religious themes is to convey a religious message or teaching. It could be a story from the religion's scripture or history, or it might be aspects of the life of a holy person that can help believers know what is expected of them.

Art produced by a religious person

A work of art may be the result of the artist wanting to express or share their religious beliefs with others. For example, many Tibetan Buddhist artists will produce thangkas (painted or embroidered linen banners) to serve as a record of, and guide for, their meditation.

Art paid for by a religious individual, group or community

It may not be the artist but the artist's client who wishes to express or share their religious beliefs with others. The client may believe that by commissioning the work of art they are showing their commitment to the religion, or that a religious message can be conveyed to others. In the past, for example, many wealthy Christians paid for altar paintings.

> **Discussion activity**
>
> 1 Look at the altar painting. Discuss: 'Paying for a painting is not the way to gain God's forgiveness for sin.' Do you agree? Give reasons for your answer, showing that you have thought about more than one point of view.

Art that produces a spiritual response

The theme of the work of art may not be specifically linked to religion, but the effect on those viewing it might be a spiritual experience. For example, Botticelli's painting of the birth of the Greek goddess Venus has influenced others to be creative and not always in the field of art. Robin Williamson's song, 'Will We Open The Heavens' (1972) is about Botticelli and mentions the painting several times.

◼ Spirituality through religious art

One way in which spirituality is expressed or experienced is through religious art. The impact religious art seeks to achieve on those producing or looking at it includes the following:

> **Objectives**
>
> Understand what is meant by religious art.
>
> Explore how religious art is produced.

> **AQA** *Examiner's tip*
>
> In the examination, you may refer to one or a combination of any of the specified religions.

> **Key terms**
>
> **Art:** range of visual images made by people, e.g. paintings, calligraphy, icon.
>
> **Inspiration:** something which stimulates or has a beneficial, uplifting effect on the mood and senses.
>
> **Revelation:** that God reveals himself through special or general revelation.
>
> **Devotion:** dedicated to something, for example to one's religion.

A *An altar painting in a Christian church*

⬭links

The term 'spirituality' is discussed in more detail on pages 8–9.

- To make people think about God or reflect on spiritual ideas.
- To convey a religious teaching.
- To express a religious belief about the 'meaning of life'.
- To help people understand spiritual truths.
- To aid worship.

Religious art can be a very effective way of expressing a spiritual message if the viewers can immediately see what the message is and, at the same time, are made to think more deeply about their beliefs.

B *Hindu painting from an Indian temple*

How is religious art produced?

Religious art may be produced for a variety of reasons, but all of these reasons are linked to religious beliefs and are the result of inspiration, revelation and/or devotion.

Inspiration

Inspiration is sometimes called 'divine **inspiration**'. Inspiration means that the artist has had a sudden idea of how the piece should look and becomes creative. Divine inspiration means that God has inspired the artist to create the work.

Revelation

In a **revelation**, the artist suddenly becomes aware of some spiritual truth previously unknown to them that they wish to share with others. They share it through their work of art.

Devotion

The artist and/or the client want to show their **devotion** to their religion, and do this through the creation of a work of art. It may be that the piece of art is intended as a focus to aid concentration during prayer and meditation, or simply as a teaching aid.

Summary

You should now be able to explain what is meant by religious art, and why it is produced.

Discussion activity

2   Discuss what each class member has written about the Hindu painting and whether or not it helps you to understand Hindu beliefs better than you did before. Record your findings.

Activity

1   Study the Hindu painting and write down what it teaches you about Hindu beliefs.

Activities

2   Explain what is meant by 'religious art'.

3   Explain **four** ways in which religious art can express a spiritual message.

4   Explain how inspiration, revelation and devotion can result in the production of religious art.

Extension activity

Using the internet and/or a library, research a piece of religious art in the religion(s) you are studying.

AQA   Examiner's tip

Make sure that you are able to explain the terms 'inspiration', 'revelation' and 'devotion'.

1.3   Icons, paintings and stained glass

◼ Symbolism in art

To understand the meaning behind any work of art, you need to understand the **symbolism**. This means working out the meaning of the work's images. The symbolism can be very important when a piece of art is meant to convey a religious message to people who cannot read. Every symbol will have been chosen to convey a meaning that the worshippers understand.

∞ links

Look back to pages 10–11 to remind yourself of what is meant by religious art.

Activity

1 Look at the painting of the Hindu god, Shiva. Before you read the case study, write down what the symbols in the painting might mean. Check your answer against the meanings given in the case study.

Case study

Shiva

In Hinduism, Shiva is responsible for the creation, preservation and destruction in the world. Shiva has three eyes to see past, present and future. Two of Shiva's four hands are to hold the balance between creation (represented by the drum) and destruction (represented by the trident). Shiva's other two hands represent salvation and protection. The serpent wrapped around his body is a reminder of the cycle of time. It has its tail in its mouth to represent infinity. Shiva is also called the Lord of the Dance and is often placed within a circle to show his responsibility for the never-ending circle of birth and death. In this painting, the artist has put a circle of light behind the god. Shiva is usually painted blue because on one occasion he swallowed poison to save the earth.

Research activity 🔍

Using the internet and/or a library, find out more about the symbols associated with Shiva.

∞ links

For other types of religious art – calligraphy, graffiti, sculpture – see pages 14–15.

◼ Icons

Icons are pictures, usually painted on wood. They show the full face of Christ, the Virgin Mary, angels and/or saints. Many are decorated with gold, silver and/or jewels. They are used mainly in the Christian Orthodox Church to teach people about God or as an aid to prayer and meditation.

Objectives

Investigate icons, paintings and stained glass as religious art.

Explore how these art forms are used.

A   *The Hindu god, Shiva*

Key terms

Symbolism: when an image or action stands for something else.

Icon: painting or mosaic of Jesus or the saints. They are more than simply aids to prayer, as they are seen as being filled with the spirit of the person shown.

B   *An icon of the Virgin Mary and Christ*

In all Orthodox churches there is a screen called the iconostasis painted with icons. The screen includes pictures of Christ, the Virgin Mary, John the Baptist and the 12 Apostles of Jesus. The icons are there to remind worshippers that it is through these holy people that they can be guided to God. Many Orthodox Christians also have icons in their homes and use them for private worship.

Paintings

Painting is applying oil paints or watercolours to a surface such as paper, wood or canvas. A painting can show either abstract shapes or a representation of the real world.

Religious painting is used as a way of representing or reminding believers of an aspect of the faith's teaching or an important holy person. For example, most Sikh temples and homes will have a painting of the founder of the faith, Guru Nanak.

C *A painting of Guru Nanak (Sikhism)*

∞ links

See pages 16–17 for an indepth study of the painting 'The Resurrection in Cookham Churchyard' by Sir Stanley Spencer.

Stained glass

Stained glass can be made by spraying different colours on to plain glass and firing it in a furnace to fuse the colour on to the glass. It can also be made by cutting coloured glass into different shapes and connecting them to make pictures or patterns.

Stained glass as religious art is most commonly found in the windows of Christian and Jewish places of worship. It may tell a story from the scriptures or commemorate a holy person or a special event.

D *Stained-glass window symbolising the Jewish Seder festival*

Activity

2 'There should be no paintings of the founders of the major religions because we do not know what they looked like.' Do you agree? Give reasons for your answer, showing that you have thought about more than one point of view.

Extension activities

1 Using the internet and/or a library, find out what happens at the Jewish Seder festival.

2 Write a description of the meaning of the symbols in the stained-glass window showing the Jewish Seder festival.

AQA Examiner's tip

Make sure that you know of examples of religious art that you can use to support your answers in the examination.

Summary

You should now be able to describe three different types of religious art and explain how each type is used.

1.4   Calligraphy, graffiti and sculpture

■ Calligraphy

The word '**calligraphy**' literally means beautiful writing. In the past, before the printing press was invented, all books were written by hand by a scribe. As these books were usually holy books, great care was taken to make them as beautiful as possible. For example, the first letter of each chapter of the Bible would be written in such a way as to explain the main theme of the chapter. Copies of the Torah used in Jewish synagogues are still written by hand today, and this is done with the greatest respect.

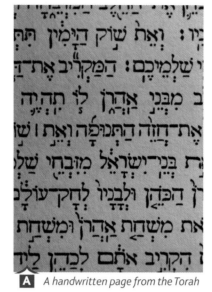

A   *A handwritten page from the Torah*

Research activity 🔍

Using the internet and/or a library, find out how calligraphy is used in copies of the Qur'an.

⬭ links

See page 20 to find out why Jews and Muslims are not allowed to have pictures and statues in their places of worship.

■ Graffiti

Graffiti is the name for images or lettering scratched, painted or marked in any manner on property. It is usually found in public places such as on walls or transport vehicles like buses. Most graffiti is considered to be an act of vandalism and against the law. However, many graffiti artists are careful about where they do their work and ask permission to use a space. Some are paid and specially commissioned because their graffiti is regarded as a form of art.

There are some religious believers who use graffiti to communicate their religious message. They may simply write a religious statement such as 'Jesus lives' or 'I am one with God' on a wall.

Discussion activity 👥

With a partner, in a small group or as a whole class, discuss whether or not you think the founder of the religion(s) you are studying would have used graffiti to make their message public if spray paint had been available at the time. Record your findings.

Objectives

Investigate calligraphy, graffiti and sculpture as religious art.

Explore how these art forms are used.

Key terms

Calligraphy: stylised writing, often associated with Islam, which turns words into beautiful pictures.

Graffiti: street art, whereby words and images are sprayed onto walls.

⬭ links

Look back to pages 12–13 to remind yourself of other types of religious art – stained glass, icons and paintings.

Activity

1   Play the video on www.gospelgraffiti.com. A Christian graffiti artist explains his beliefs as he creates a piece of religious graffiti.

■ Sculpture

Sculpture is three-dimensional artwork that is created by shaping materials such as stone (either rock or marble), metal, wood, plastic or other materials. Some sculptures are created directly by carving, while others are assembled from sections that are moulded or fired together. As with the other forms of religious art, sculpture is intended to convey a religious message. The sculpture may depict a recognisable figure, event or, in the case of Judaism or Islam, it may be decorative work, for example, to enhance the beauty of a place of worship.

B *A statue of the Buddha*

C *The Angel of the North*

Activity

2 'Spending £1m on the sculpture of an angel was a waste of money.' Do you agree? Give reasons for your answer, showing that you have thought about more than one point of view.

Case study

The Angel of the North

The Angel of the North was constructed from weather-resistant steel in 1998. It cost £1m and was financed by the National Lottery. It has become a landmark in the North of England and is visible from the A1 road. It is the world's largest angel sculpture, and its wingspan is almost equal to that of a jumbo jet. The sculptor, Antony Gormley, stated that, 'The angel has three functions: firstly a historic one to remind us that below the site coal miners worked in the dark for 200 years, secondly to grasp hold of the future expressing our transition from the industrial to the information age, and lastly to be a focus for our hopes and fears.'

Activities

3 Describe **three** types of religious art.

4 'Religious art is a good way to spread a religious message.' Do you agree? Give reasons for your answer, showing that you have thought about more than one point of view.

AQA Examiner's tip

Remember that you need to know examples of religious art that you can use to support your answers in the examination.

Summary

You should now be able to describe three different types of religious art, and explain how each type is used to express spirituality.

1.5 The Resurrection in Cookham Churchyard – a case study

◼ How was the painting produced?

The Resurrection in Cookham Churchyard was painted by Sir Stanley Spencer (1891–1959) and can now be seen in the Tate Gallery in London. A large oil painting on canvas, 9ft high by 18ft wide, it took from 1924 to 1926 to complete.

A *The Resurrection in Cookham Churchyard*

Inspiration

Spencer's inspiration came from what he called 'a visionary experience' and meeting with his future wife, Hilda Carlines. Hilda raised such 'wonderful thoughts' in him, and this experience resulted in the painting with a resurrection theme. He felt that the only place to set his painting was the churchyard of Cookham village, in Kent. He had grown up in Cookham and had a happy childhood there.

Revelation

This 'vision' that Spencer experienced was two-fold. His love for Hilda made him very happy and, through this happiness, he became aware of what paradise would be like because, as he said, he felt that 'God is Love'.

Discussion activity 👤👤👤

'God is Love', is a quote from St John's Gospel in the Christian New Testament.

1 Discuss what you think is meant by 'God is Love'. Do you agree? Give reasons for your answer, showing that you have thought about more than one point of view.

Beliefs and teachings

Part of the Christian Statement of Belief

I believe in the Holy Spirit,
the holy catholic church,
the communion of saints,
the forgiveness of sins;
the resurrection of the body,
and life everlasting.

The Apostles' Creed

Devotion

Spencer was a Christian who accepted the Christian belief that, at the end of time, Christ would return, raise the dead and lead them to heaven. Spencer believed that throughout the world it was possible to see evidence of God's creation in the ordinary everyday things, and he wanted to share this knowledge and understanding with others.

Activities

1 Briefly describe the painting *The Resurrection in Cookham Churchyard* or choose another painting from a religious tradition you are studying.

2 Explain what may have influenced the artist to paint the work.

3 'The painting has a religious message.' Do you agree? Give reasons for your answer, showing that you have thought about more than one point of view.

Discussion activity

2 As a whole class, discuss what Spencer might be trying to say through the things he has painted in the picture. Record your findings.

The symbolism of the painting

The Resurrection in Cookham Churchyard is a very detailed painting, full of symbols and images. Spencer has used a real churchyard as the setting and all the figures in the painting are actual people that he knew and loved. Spencer has put himself in the painting as the naked figure leaning next to two gravestones. For Spencer, the resurrection is a real event.

Christ has returned and is sitting on a throne in the church porch, and behind him stands God. Along the church wall is a row of prophets including Moses, with a dark beard, holding the tablets of the Ten Commandments.

Among the dead rising from the graves are black as well as white figures. In this way, Spencer is showing that the resurrection is for all. He believes that everyone will get to heaven, but it will be more difficult for the sinners to leave their graves, and so it will take them longer to get there.

As they rise, the figures are looking at their own headstones, which are circular. One suggestion as to why Spencer chose a circular form is that it links to the Hindu wheel of life because he had an interest in Eastern religions.

The risen dead are taken to heaven on the pleasure steamers working on the Thames. For Spencer, as for all Christians, the resurrection is an event to be celebrated.

Summary

You should now have an insight into the symbolism and effect of a painting and be able to discuss this.

links

Look back to page 11 to remind yourself of how religious art is produced.

Research activity

Using the internet and/or a library, find out more about Sir Stanley Spencer's other paintings with biblical themes.

AQA Examiner's tip

You need to be able to discuss at least one piece of art for the examination. It can be taken from any of the six religions.

links

Look back to page 12 to remind yourself of what is meant by the symbolism of a painting.

B *The Hindu wheel of life*

Activity

4 a Look closely at *The Resurrection in Cookham Churchyard*. Make a list of all the different things you can see happening in the painting.

b Compare your list with what other people in your class have seen in the painting.

1.6 How and why religions use art

How religions use art

The major religions of the world use art in a number of ways:

- an act of devotion
- a teaching aid
- an aid to prayer
- a way of making others aware of the religion.

An act of devotion

For some believers, creating or commissioning a work of art is an act of devotion. For example, the writing of the holy book by hand was, and still is, regarded as an act of devotion, as is reading the teachings contained within the book.

The sacred writings of each faith are the basis of the religion's beliefs. The importance of the writings is shown by their physical appearance as works of great beauty – not only by the calligraphy used but by the use of decoration. For example, because Muslims believe the Qur'an to be the direct Word of Allah, the importance of the book may be emphasised by decoration.

A teaching aid

Art can be a teaching aid, especially for people who cannot read. The stories and teachings from the sacred writings and the lives of the holy people who have helped to shape the faith can be explained to believers visually through stained-glass windows, paintings and sculpture.

In Christian churches, stained-glass windows often outline the life of a saint or a story from the Bible. In Judaism, windows in synagogues may show sacred objects such as the menorah, the seven or eight-branched candelabrum as instructed in the book of Exodus.

Objectives

Investigate how and why religions use art.

⊙⊙ links

Look back to pages 12–15 to remind yourself of the different types of religious art.

A The Qur'an is believed by Muslims to be the direct Word of Allah

Activity

1 Study the stained-glass window and read the parable of the lost sheep (Luke 15:4–7) in the New Testament. Write an explanation of how the artist has taught the story in the window.

B Stained-glass window telling the Parable of the Lost Sheep

C A stone carving of Hindu gods on a temple wall

Sculpture and painting can also be used to illustrate religious teachings or an aspect of the life of a holy person. There may be separate paintings, statues or carvings into the stone or bricks in a place of worship.

An aid to prayer

Art can also be used as an aid to prayer and meditation. People pray before icons of the Virgin Mary and saints asking them to speak to God on their behalf. Buddhist temples have a painting or a statue of the Buddha as the focus of prayer and meditation; Hindu temples have images of the gods and goddesses to which the temple is dedicated; and in Catholic churches there will be a statue of the Virgin Mary, sometimes in a chapel dedicated to her.

To make others aware of the religion

Pieces of art, in the form of symbols, can be used to identify the religion on the exterior of a place of worship. For example, Sikhs will often have the Sikh emblem (the nishan sahib) on the wall above the main entrance, whereas synogogues will have the Star of David (the Magen David).

Many believers show the importance of their beliefs by wearing a religious symbol, which is often formed into a piece of jewellery.

◯◯ links

See pages 12–13 to find out more about icons.

Extension activity

Using the internet and/or a library, find other examples of symbols used to identify the religion(s) you are studying.

▮ Why religions use art

Religions use art as an effective way of expressing a spiritual message. Unless it is abstract, the believer can immediately see what the art is about and use it to think further about the meaning of their faith.

Some believers use art to express their love of God or their religion. Religious graffiti may be created because the believer feels so strongly about their faith at a particular moment that they need to share this strong emotion with others.

Art is also a way of spreading the religion's message to members of other religions or non-believers. One reason why people are allowed to visit places of worship is that by looking at the religious art, they may become aware of a power greater than themselves, and may even experience a conversion to that religion.

◯◯ links

See pages 14–15 to find out more about religious graffiti.

Activities

2   Explain **three** reasons why religions use art, giving examples.

3   'A beautiful piece of religious art could convert people to that religion.' Do you agree? Give reasons for your answer, showing that you have thought about more than one point of view.

Summary

You should now be able to explain how and why religions use art.

AQA   Examiner's tip

Make sure that you are able to support your answers with examples.

1.7 How religious art is used in worship

How religious art is used in public worship

Public worship is open to all and occurs when the followers of a specific religion come together for worship, usually in a place of worship. How religious art is used in public worship will depend on what is acceptable as an art form to the religion.

Islam

A There are no images of people or animals in a mosque

To have statues and art representing humans and animals in a mosque or the home is considered to be blasphemy by Islam. As only Allah is the creator of living things, it is wrong to try to imitate them in art. This form of art is also forbidden for fear that its presence could lead to the worship of idols.

Instead, the walls of a mosque are decorated with calligraphy – usually sections from the Qur'an in Arabic or the 99 names for Allah to remind worshippers of the Word of Allah. Another form of decoration used is geometric designs, often free flowing, floral or tree-shaped, with lines, curves and angles that blend together. Loud or vivid colours are avoided as the aim is to make the mosque a beautiful and restful place of worship.

In both public and private worship, the Qur'an is central to worship. Therefore, the main use of religious art is to stress the beauty of the Qur'an as the Word of Allah and the perfection of the nature of Allah through symmetrical patterns.

Judaism

There are no representations of humans or animals in synagogues as this would break the second commandment from God not to have images. Decoration is restricted to extracts from the Torah or simple designs such as patterns or flowers.

As with Islam, in Judaism it is the 'words' of the message that are important and this is why calligraphy is the main art form used to support worship.

AQA Examiner's tip

Make sure that you understand the views of the religion(s) you are studying about the use of art in public worship.

links

Look back to page 9 to remind yourself of your research on what is meant by blasphemy.

links

Look back to page 14 and remind yourself of what is meant by calligraphy.

Beliefs and teachings

The second commandment

You shall not make for yourself an idol in the form of anything in heaven above or on the earth beneath or in the waters below. You shall not bow down to them or worship them.

Exodus 20:4–5

Buddhism, Christianity, Hinduism and Sikhism

All these religions allow humans and animals to be portrayed in art forms within their places of worship. But, as with Islam and Judaism, the main use of religious art in worship is to direct the worshippers to the central beliefs of the faith or to support prayer and meditation. For example, when a Sikh looks at a painting of Guru Nanak, the founder of Sikhism, they are reminded of his teachings and from this may think about how they should put those teachings into practice. A painting above an altar in a Christian church is a reminder of Christ's sacrifice on the cross and the link with the service of Holy Communion. Sikhs and Christians would not use the pictures as 'idols' and their presence is seen as a sign of respect for the people depicted.

Activities

1. Explain why neither Islam nor Judaism has images of humans or animals in their places of worship.

2. Describe **two** ways in which religious art is used in a public place of worship and give examples.

How religious art is used in private worship

Private worship usually takes place in the home. In private worship, the use of religious art may help individuals feel closer to God and more able to communicate directly with him, or, in the case of Buddhism, feel closer to achieving understanding of the meaning of life.

In those religions that allow human images, a statue or painting may help concentration during prayer and meditation. For example, many Catholics have a statue of the Virgin Mary or a saint in their homes as an aid to prayer. Buddhists may have a statue or painting of the Buddha and Hindus may have statues or paintings of the gods and goddesses.

Research activity

2. Using the internet and/or a library, find some more examples of how religious art is used in public or private worship in the religion(s) you have studied.

Activities

3. Describe **two** ways in which religious art is used in private worship and give examples.

4. 'It does not matter what you use as an aid to worship so long as you worship.' Do you agree? Give reasons for your answer, showing that you have thought about more than one point of view.

Research activity

1. Using the internet and/or a library, find out what the link is in Christianity between the symbol of the cross and the service of Holy Communion.

Discussion activity

As a whole class, discuss whether or not it is important to have a richly decorated place of worship. Record your findings.

B *In Hinduism, praying to the elephant god, Ganesha, is thought to bring good fortune*

Summary

You should now be able to explain how religious art is used in public and private worship.

1.8 The impact of religious art

The intended impact

Religious art is intended to make people think about God or religious truth, or to remind them of religious teachings. It is hoped that the art will help them to understand the religious message within it.

However, religious art could actually put someone off a religion if it is felt that the image or message is too harsh – for example, if the message seems unacceptable or too frightening to think about.

The impact of religious art on believers is likely to be different from the impact on non-believers because of the different understanding(s) they will have about the message conveyed. Although non-believers may not accept the teachings of a religion, they can still experience a spiritual response to the beauty of art or the message it conveys. For example, they may feel a sense of peace when looking at a painting of a holy figure or fear when looking at a picture of sinners going to hell.

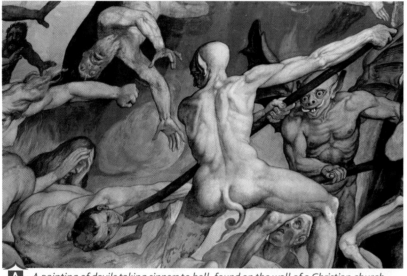

A *A painting of devils taking sinners to hell, found on the wall of a Christian church*

AQA *Examiner's tip*

Remember to think about the influence of spirituality on believers and non-believers.

Discussion activity

Study the painting of devils taking sinners to hell. It is a reminder that if people sin they will go to hell as a punishment.

1 Discuss whether or not such religious art is more likely to make you follow the teaching of the religion. Record your findings.

The impact of religious art on believers

When a believer looks at religious art from their own religion, they are likely to understand the message that it contains. As a result, they are likely to have an emotional response, making them think more deeply about their religious beliefs. It may make the believer feel great love of God or, in the case of Buddhism, closer to achieving enlightenment.

For example, in the Orthodox Church, icons are reminders of the spiritual world and regarded as a 'window to heaven'. The icon of Christ supports the Christian belief that God came into the world in the human form of Jesus. The icons themselves are not worshipped, but being reminded of God and heaven will often produce feelings of joy and love so great that an individual might kiss an icon.

Art as blasphemy

Sometimes, however, art can shock the believer and cause offence because the image is seen as blasphemy. In some cases, believers have felt so strongly that an image is an insult to their religion that they protest – sometimes violently.

links

Look back to pages 12–13 to remind yourself of what is meant by an icon.

You can find a definition of blasphemy in the Glossary.

Case study

Wikipedia's images of Muhammad

Muslims consider that it is blasphemy to produce images of Muhammad. This is because they believe only Allah can create life and there is fear that the image will be worshipped instead of Allah. When it was discovered that Wikipedia, the free online encyclopaedia, contained images of Muhammad, there was an outcry. Many Muslims wanted the images removed, whereas many non-Muslims argued that they should remain as they did not find them offensive. The editors of the encyclopaedia said that they would not bow to pressure and if people objected to the images, they could adjust their computers so that they did not have to look at them. Wikipedia said, 'Since Wikipedia is an encyclopaedia with the goal of representing all topics from a neutral point of view, Wikipedia is not censored for the benefit of any particular group.'

links

See pages 82–83 for reactions to the publication of other images of Muhammad.

Activity

1   Explain the impact religious art might have on a believer, in a positive or negative way.

The impact of religious art on non-believers

Most non-believers cannot understand why there could be an outcry about paintings of the founder of a religion. Many atheists may consider the disagreement between different religions about what is acceptable in art to be further evidence that God does not exist because, if he did, then the religions would all share the same view.

Sometimes religious art can change people's view about religion. Religious graffiti, for example, is displayed in public places with the aim of making others aware of a religious belief. It is hoped that the graffiti will encourage people to think about their way of life and how they can improve it spiritually.

B   *Religious graffiti can make people think about their beliefs*

Discussion activity

2   With a partner, in a small group or as a whole class, discuss whether or not the message on graffiti on a bridge over the motorway could lead to someone changing their way of life. Record your findings.

Activities

2   Explain the impact that religious art might have on a non-believer.
3   'It's OK to have pictures of religious figures if you are a non-believer.' Do you agree? Give reasons for your answer, showing that you have thought about more than one point of view.

Summary

You should now be able to describe and explain the impact of religious art on both believers and non-believers.

1.9 What does religious art tell us about God, belief and the artist?

◼ What does religious art tell us about God?

Many believers argue that the very fact that people are inspired to create pieces of religious art is evidence that God does exist. They argue that there is some part of God within people that results in the desire to be creative – or it may be the beauty of God's creation that leads them to express this beauty through art. Buddhists do not believe in God: therefore, Buddhist artists produce works that focus on the meaning of life. However, such artists will also see their art as an expression of their spirituality.

Muslims and Jews would argue that religious art cannot tell people about Allah/God himself as he is beyond human understanding. For them, the purpose of religious art is to show the beauty of Allah's/God's message and this is why calligraphy is used.

Beliefs and teachings

The 99 beautiful names of Allah

The most beautiful names belong to Allah: so call on Him by them; but shun such men as distort His names: for what they do, they will soon be requited [punished].

Qur'an 7:180

A *The name of Allah in Arabic script*

Research activity 🔍

Muslims believe that it is not possible to understand Allah, but that as a help to understanding him there are 99 names of Allah in the Qur'an. Using the internet and/or a library, find out more about these 99 beautiful names.

◼ What does religious art tell us about belief?

In Islam and Judaism, religious art is mainly concerned with beautifying the words that are the basis of their beliefs. This includes not only words from their holy books, but also the teachings from religious leaders.

The other religions also display texts from their sacred books or teachings from holy people. However, they also use paintings and sculptures to show what the belief means and how it can be put into practice. Such a piece of art may show a story from a holy book, a historical event from the religion's past or a religious belief put into practice. Through such reminders, those looking at the picture are challenged to think about their beliefs. They will sometimes also remember how old their faith is and how many different people have shared their beliefs.

B *The Ten Gurus are shown with haloes*

What does religious art tell us about the artist?

This depends on the reasons why the artist created the piece of art. If it was as a commission for somebody else, it might only tell us that the artist was creating a piece of art for money. Yet, many artists will not take on work that does not relate to their beliefs, or may refuse a commission because they feel they could not express the understanding of the faith in their art that others might expect. To really understand what religious art tells us about the artist, it is probably necessary to know something about the artist's life and religious beliefs.

It may be that the more the artist is inspired by genuine religious beliefs to create the piece of religious art, the more the work will be successful in expressing religious beliefs and having an impact on those who see their work.

C   *A wood carving of the story of Rama and Sita*

D   *What does this painting by the artist Michelangelo tell us about his religious beliefs?*

Summary

You should now be able to explain what religious art tells us about God, belief and the artist.

1.10 The symbolic nature of religious art and its place in the modern world

◼ The symbolic nature of religious art

All religions use symbols to convey messages related to their beliefs. Members of a religion are able to recognise the symbols of their religion and explain their underlying meaning. As a result, the symbol can often produce a spiritual response that leads the individual to think more deeply about the religion. This can be seen in the way in which Christians use the symbols of the cross and the crucifix in their public and private worship. It can also be seen in the **symbolism** associated with each of the Hindu gods and goddesses.

Objectives

Investigate the symbolic nature of religious art.

Investigate the place of religious art in the modern world.

Key terms

Symbolism: when an image or action stands for something else.

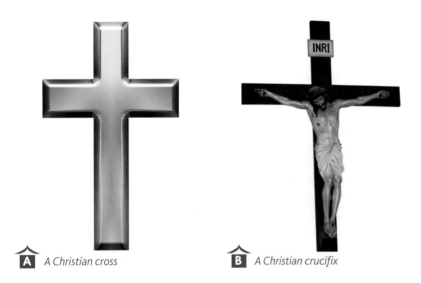

A *A Christian cross*

B *A Christian crucifix*

⊙⊙ **links**

Look back to pages 12–15 to remind yourself of the link between religious symbols and religious art.

The Christian cross and crucifix

Case study

Most Christian places of worship display either a cross or a crucifix as a symbol of the Christian belief that Jesus died on the cross to save them from God's punishment for sin. Many Christians will use either a cross or a crucifix as an aid to private prayer and meditation.

Although both the cross and the crucifix are reminders of Jesus' death, Christians have a different understanding of the meaning behind each symbol.

An empty cross reminds Christians that through his sacrifice, Jesus conquered sin and death. Christians hope that by following Jesus they will achieve eternal life with God after death. An empty cross helps Christians concentrate on what may be the rewards of following Jesus and being obedient to God.

A crucifix includes the body of Christ nailed to the cross. It is used to remind Christians of the suffering of Jesus on the cross to gain forgiveness from God for the sins of the world.

⊙⊙ **links**

Look back to pages 8–9 to remind yourself of what is meant by spirituality.

◼ The place of religious art in the modern world

Most religions argue that religious art is a very effective way of expressing a spiritual message, especially as there are still many places in the world where people are unable to read the religious texts for themselves. Some believers would argue that art does not have to be drawn from a religious perspective to make someone think about religious truths. The painting of a beautiful landscape or a sunset could arouse feelings of wonder and evoke a spiritual response.

Many atheists would deny that there is any place for religious art in the modern world as the world is becoming secular. This is because fewer and fewer people attend a place of worship. As people no longer learn about the teachings of religion, the symbols and messages contained within pieces of religious art do not mean anything to them.

C   *Does this painting of a stormy ocean make you think there is a power greater than yourself?*

Not all art with a religious theme is religious. The way in which the subject matter is used could be disrespectful to God or the religion and, as a result, be regarded as blasphemous. The aim of the art may be to deny the existence of God or an underlying meaning to life.

There are other artists who seek to show that religion has declined in modern society. The theme might be abandoned places of worship, to show that they believe we are becoming a secular world and that there is a decline or end of faith in the world.

Research activities 🔍

1   Using the internet and/or a library, find out about one of the following Hindu gods:

- ◼ Brahma
- ◼ Shiva
- ◼ Vishnu.

2   Find out what symbols would be used to portray the god and what the symbols mean.

D   *Does this picture of an abandoned church have a religious message?*

Activities

1   Explain what is meant by the symbolic nature of religious art.
2   'There is no place for religious art in the modern world.' Do you agree? Give reasons for your answer, showing that you have thought about more than one point of view.

Summary

You should now be able to explain the symbolic nature of religious art and evaluate its contribution to spirituality in the modern world.

AQA   *Examiner's tip*

Remember, you should always support your answers with examples from the religion(s) you have studied.

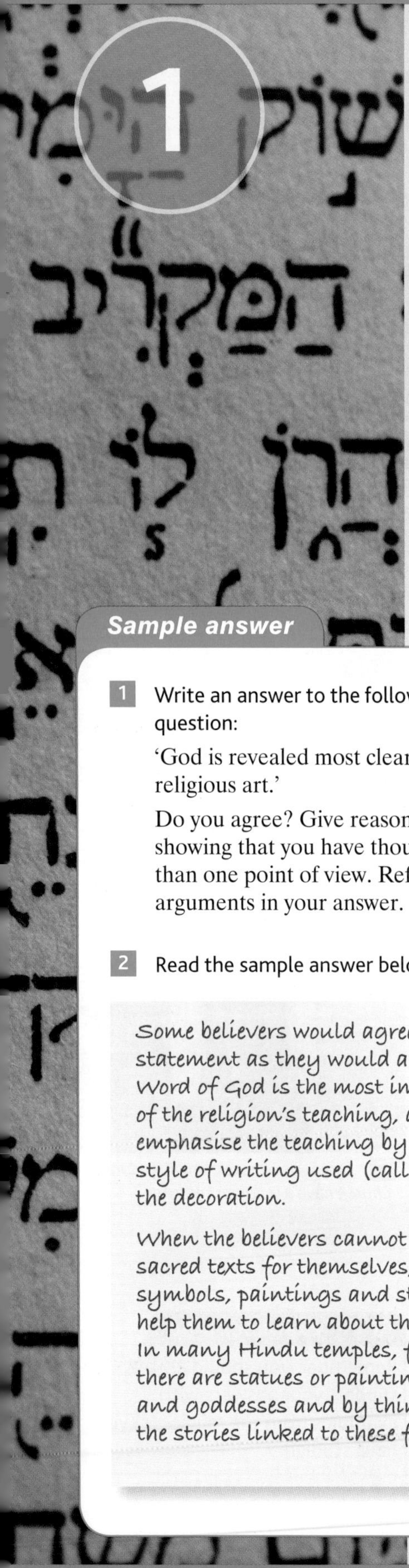

① Religion and art – summary

For the examination you should now be able to:

✔ describe and explain what is meant by 'spirituality'

✔ describe and explain what is meant by 'religious art'

✔ describe and explain different types of religious art including icons, painting, calligraphy and sculpture

✔ describe and explain how and why religions use art

✔ explain how religious art is used in public and private worship

✔ explain the impact that religious art has on those looking on – believers and non-believers

✔ explain what religious art tells us about God, belief and the artist

✔ explain the symbolic nature of this form of spirituality

✔ evaluate the place of religious art as a way of expressing spirituality in the modern world.

Sample answer

1 Write an answer to the following examination question:

'God is revealed most clearly through religious art.'

Do you agree? Give reasons for your answer, showing that you have thought about more than one point of view. Refer to religious arguments in your answer.

(6 marks)

2 Read the sample answer below:

Some believers would agree with this statement as they would argue that the Word of God is the most important part of the religion's teaching, and art can emphasise the teaching by either the style of writing used (calligraphy) or the decoration.

When the believers cannot read the sacred texts for themselves, then symbols, paintings and statues can help them to learn about the religion. In many Hindu temples, for example, there are statues or paintings of the gods and goddesses and by thinking about the stories linked to these figures, the worshipper is reminded of what they are to believe and how they are to behave. Muslims and Jews would not agree with this view, as they would argue that such images could lead to mistaken beliefs and the worshipping of idols instead of Allah/God.

Other people might think that because there are different views about the way in which religious art is used, it shows that there are contradictions about what people should believe. Also, if you do not know the meaning behind a symbol, then the religious art does not mean anything to you.

I think that because fewer people are learning about religion, then the religious art will not teach them about God.

3 With a partner, discuss the sample answer. Do you think that there are other things that the student could have included in the answer?

4 What mark would you give this answer out of 6? (Look at the mark scheme in the Introduction on page 7 (AO2) before you attempt this.) What are the reasons for the mark you have given?

AQA Examination-style questions

1 Look at the photograph and answer the following questions.

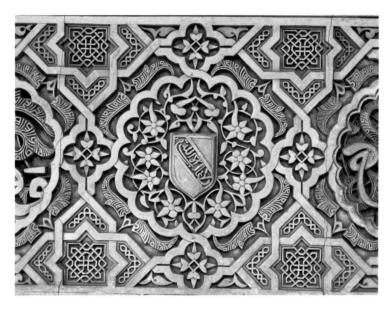

(a) Explain what is meant by 'spirituality'. *(2 marks)*

You need to give a full explanation of the word, making either two points or a development of one point. Give an example if it helps to explain the word.

(b) Explain briefly why religious believers use religious art to support their religious beliefs. *(3 marks)*

You need to show that you understand how religious art is used to support religious beliefs. Referring to examples of how religious art is used may help you.

(c) Explain the impact of **one** type of religious art you have studied. *(4 marks)*

You could explain the impact on believers and/or non-believers.

(d) 'It's wrong to have paintings of people in places of worship.'
What do you think? Explain your opinion. *(3 marks)*

Even if you are asked for your opinion, you will actually get marks for the **reasons** you give. Write one well-developed reason or several simple ones.

(e) 'God must exist because art is inspired by God.' Do you agree? Give reasons for your answer, showing that you have thought about more than one point of view. Refer to religious arguments in your answer. *(6 marks)*

The final question is worth the most marks. Before you start writing, think carefully of reasons why some people think God must exist because art is inspired by God, and why other people think it is not.

2 Religion and architecture

2.1 What is architecture?

Defining architecture

Architecture is the activity of designing and constructing buildings and other physical structures, using people and machines. Buildings and structures are built for a wide variety of reasons and functions. The functions of buildings include:

- worship
- living and working
- education
- celebration
- leisure activities.

Objectives

Investigate what is meant by 'architecture' and the influence of spirituality on architecture.

Key terms

Architecture: buildings, statues.

Activity

1 a Copy the bullet-point list above and use it to identify the different functions of buildings in the village/town/city where you live.

   b As you find them, note down the type of building used for each function.

   c Add any other buildings you see with different functions.

The influences on architecture

The influence of function

When designing a building, the architect has to think about what its function will be. Some buildings may serve more than one function, for example a place of worship may also be used for social activities or a community centre may be used for both leisure and educational activities.

A *We all need somewhere to live*

B *Different countries and periods in history have different designs for the same structure*

The design of the building will be influenced not only by the function of the building, but also by building fashion at the time it is built, the materials available, or by the laws, customs, weather and wealth of the country in which it is built. The design of a building with the same function may change throughout history.

The use of a building may change through time because its original function is no longer needed. An old cinema may become a warehouse or bingo hall, an old mill may become a block of flats, or an old school building could become a place of worship.

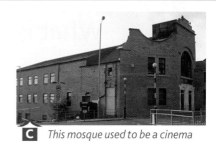

C This mosque used to be a cinema

The influence of spirituality

Another influence on architecture or architects is spirituality. It may be that an individual or a community commissions a building or structure to express something of spiritual importance to them. It may be that the architect wishes to express a spiritual message through their work. When others see the architectural work, they often feel emotions that could be described as spiritual – such as joy, awe or sadness.

D How has spirituality influenced this structure?

Remember, the individual's response to the work may be spiritual, but it may not be religious. Individuals can have spiritual experiences without accepting the teachings of a religious tradition. Certain architecture may make them feel that there is a deeper meaning to life or a power greater than themselves.

links

Look back to pages 8–9 to remind yourself of what is meant by spirituality.

AQA *Examiner's tip*

Make sure that you understand the relationship between spirituality and architecture because you may be asked to discuss it in the examination.

E Places of worship do contribute to spirituality

Discussion activity

Look at the photograph of the war memorial above. Discuss the spiritual message you think has influenced the design of this structure. Record your findings.

Activities

2 Explain what is meant by 'architecture'.

3 Describe briefly the function of **three** different buildings.

4 Explain how spirituality influences architecture.

Summary

You should now be able to explain what is meant by 'architecture' and the influence of spirituality upon it.

2.2   What is religious architecture?

Defining religious architecture

Religious architecture refers to buildings and structures that in some way try to express both a religious and spiritual message. It includes places where specific acts of religious praise, honour or devotion take place, although it may be that not all activities that take place within such a building are religious. Religious architecture could be a specific building designed as a place of worship, a shrine or a structure to commemorate a place or person important to the religion. It may be a place to which religious believers can withdraw from everyday life, such as a monastery. It may be a large, ornate building or a small simple space. It could be designed for public worship or private use.

The type and design of religious architecture vary from religion to religion, to suit the particular beliefs and needs for worship. The design may need to include areas of peace, calm and simplicity or rooms for specific purposes, such as a room in which the Guru Granth Sahib (the Sikh holy book) is literally put to bed at night in Sikh gurdwaras.

Research activity

1.   Find **three** examples of religious architecture in your locality. Write a description of the type and design of each one.

A   *The Vatican was built as the residence of the Pope and the administrative centre of the Catholic Church*

B   *Buddhist monasteries have areas designed for exercise and study*

Discussion activity

Some religious buildings are given grants by a goverment to help maintain them:

1.   With a partner, in a small group or as a whole class, discuss the following statement: 'I don't go to any places of worship, so I shouldn't have to pay for their upkeep.' Do you agree? Give reasons for your answer, showing that you have thought about more than one point of view.

▌ Spirituality through religious architecture

C   *Many people have had a spiritual experience looking at the Taj Mahal*

∞ links

Look back to pages 8–9 to make sure that you understand what is meant by spirituality.

Research activity

2   Using the internet find out more about the reasons why the Taj Mahal was originally built.

Look at the impact that religious architecture seeks to achieve and decide which features from the list the Taj Mahal achieves.

A building or structure may not be specifically linked to a religion, but the effects on those viewing the structure might result in a spiritual experience because of the beauty or size of the building. The architecture makes them aware of a power greater than themselves or some aspect of the meaning of life.

The impact that religious architecture seeks to achieve on those producing or looking at it includes the following:

- to make people think about God or reflect on spiritual ideas
- to remind people that there is an afterlife
- to express a religious belief about achieving reward in the afterlife
- to help people understand spiritual truths
- to aid worship
- to produce a feeling of awe, grandeur and splendour.

Religious architecture can be a very effective way of expressing a spiritual message if the viewers can immediately see what the message is and, at the same time, are made to think more deeply about their beliefs.

Discussion activity ●●●

2   a   Study the photograph of a place of worship and write down what it tells you about the beliefs of the people who worship there.

b   With a partner, discuss what each of you has written.

c   Discuss whether or not the design of the place of worship has helped you understand the religious beliefs and practices of the religion that uses it. Record your findings.

D   *A place of worship*

Summary

You should now be able to explain what is meant by religious architecture, and the contribution of architecture to spirituality.

How is religious architecture produced?

As with religious art, religious architecture may be produced for a variety of reasons, but these are all linked to religious beliefs and are the result of inspiration, revelation and/or devotion.

Inspiration

Inspiration is sometimes called 'divine inspiration'. One of the purposes of religious architecture is to inspire people visiting the sacred place. It is intended that the design will make them think of God or, in the case of Buddhists, the reality of the universe.

It may be that the religious beliefs of a person or group inspire them to have a place of worship or religious structure built as an expression of their faith; or it may be the architect's beliefs that have inspired the design of the building.

The design of a building or structure can be influential in inspiring the design of later religious architecture. For example, the 1960s building of Coventry Cathedral was inspired by the earlier medieval cathedral next to it.

Revelation

Some religious architecture is the result of revelation. It may be that a particular person believes that they have been told that a building should be erected at a specific place. For example, St Bernadette had a vision of the Virgin Mary who told her that a church should be built at a specific site in Lourdes. The Sikh Golden Temple at Amritsar, also known as Harmandir Sahib, was the design of Guru Arjan Dev, who wanted a building at a level lower than the surrounding land to emphasise the inner strength provided by Sikhism.

The intention of the design of religious architecture may be to reveal something about the religion to others, and perhaps even to convert people to the religion through the feelings of awe and wonder they experience on entering the building. For example, the size or beauty of the building might make a person feel the majesty of God and, as a result, want to find out more about him.

Places where the founders of the religions have had specific revelations are also usually marked by a piece of religious architecture.

Objectives

Investigate how religious architecture is produced.

◌◌ links

Look back to page 11 to remind yourself of what is meant by inspiration.

AQA　Examiner's tip

Make sure that you are able to explain the terms 'inspiration', 'revelation' and 'devotion'.

◌◌ links

See pages 40–41 to find out more about Coventry Cathedral.

A　*Sikh Golden Temple*

◌◌ links

Look back to page 11 to remind yourself of what is meant by revelation.

The Dome of the Rock

One night, Muhammad was woken up by the Angel Jibril (Gabriel), and taken on a winged horse called al-Buraq to Jerusalem. When they reached a place near the rock on which Solomon's Temple had stood, Muhammad knelt in prayer. He then stood on the rock and was taken to heaven, where he was given the command to pray five times a day. He was taken up through the different heavens and eventually was allowed to see paradise. Muhammad was taken home before dawn.

In 685 CE, work began on building a structure that covers the sacred rock where Muhammad stood. The gold dome is covered in real gold, and stretches 20 metres over the Dome of the Rock, as the building became known. Later the al-Aqsa mosque was built nearby. When Muslims look at the Dome of the Rock, they are reminded of the revelations received by Muhammad and the importance of these revelations to them.

B   *The Dome of the Rock in Jerusalem*

Activity

1   a   Divide the class into six groups. Each group chooses one of the following places at which a revelation was received:

- Bodh Gaya (Buddhism)
- Mount of Beatitudes (Christianity)
- Varanasi (Hinduism)
- Masjid al Nabawi (Islam)
- Western Wailing Wall (Judaism)
- Golden temple of Amritsar (Sikhism)

b   Research your chosen place. Remember to think about the importance of the revelation.

c   Present your findings to the class using presentation software.

Devotion

Not only is religious architecture used for places of worship, but the actual construction of the building is also regarded by many believers as an act of devotion. The time, care and money spent on the building can demonstrate the importance of the beliefs to those involved, and to others.

The structure may not only be a place of devotion for a religious community, but also a place of personal or private prayer and meditation. The design of the building will take this need into account.

∞ links

Look back to page 11 to remind yourself of what is meant by devotion.

C   *The Western (Wailing) Wall is a place of prayer for Jews*

Activities

2   Explain what is meant by 'religious architecture'.

3   Explain ways in which religious architecture can express a spiritual message.

4   Explain how inspiration, revelation and devotion can result in the production of religious architecture.

Summary

You should now be able to explain what is meant by religious architecture, how it is produced and the influence it has on spirituality.

What is meant by a public place of worship?

Public places of worship are for specific acts of religious praise, honour or devotion where the community of believers can come together. The religious architecture of the place of worship may be a specific building or a shrine. The acts of worship that take place there are usually directed to God. Buddhists do not worship God but during acts of worship pray and meditate to gain spiritual knowledge and understanding.

Buildings as public places of worship

The architecture of buildings used as public places of worship varies according to the beliefs and form of worship of the religion using them. Even within one religion there might be differences in the designs chosen by different communities. However, there will always be certain features incorporated in the design that are essential to the specific form of worship within a religion.

The names used for buildings used as public places of worship in the religions we are studying are:

- temple – Buddhism
- chapel, church or cathedral – Christianity
- mandir (temple) – Hinduism
- mosque – Islam
- synagogue – Judaism
- gurdwara (temple) – Sikhism.

The architecture of both the interior and the exterior of the building will be designed to show that it is a place of worship, as well as to assist worship.

Exterior features

There may be a sign outside showing the name and purpose of the building and symbols associated with the religion. For example, a Sikh gurdwara is recognisable by the Sikh flag flying with the nishan sahib (the Sikh emblem). There may be accepted architectural features outside, such as a belfry, minaret or stupa.

Internal features

Inside, the architecture will be appropriate to the religion's form of worship. For example, Christian churches include an altar; Jewish synagogues house the Ark and bimah (reading desk); and in a Sikh gurdwara there is a takht (raised platform) for the Sikh holy book, the Guru Granth Sahib.

Objectives

Investigate public places of worship as a form of religious architecture.

AQA   *Examiner's tip*

Make sure that you are able to name the places of worship for the religions you have studied.

A   *Purpose-built mosques have a minaret*

Activity

1   Research the features of the place(s) of worship you are studying and explain their importance.

Shrines as public places of worship

Sometimes the place of worship may be a shrine at a holy or sacred place where people worship. It may be built at a place where something important happened within the tradition of the religion, such as a miracle, or where there are relics or the tomb of a person important to the religion. Sometimes shrines may be found within religious buildings. A stupa is an example of a shrine frequently found in Buddhist places of worship. Believers meditate or make offerings at stupas, which contain relics of the Buddha or past Buddhas.

Other public places of worship

Some people feel that the best place to worship is in the open air and that the only architecture required is that created by nature.

B   *The Golden Stupa in Bangkok*

C   *Sometimes people worship in the open air*

Activity

2   Write a detailed explanation of how religious architecture is used to support worship, giving specific examples.

Extension activity

Find an example of another shrine built to remember an event or miracle important to a particular religion.

∞ links

Look back to page 35 to see a picture of the Western (Wailing) Wall.

Case study

The Western (Wailing) Wall in Jerusalem

The Western Wall is all that remains on the site of two Jewish temples – the Temple of Solomon and Herod's Temple. The Temple of Solomon housed the Ark of the Covenant, the sacred chest containing the tablets inscribed with the Ten Commandments that were given to Moses by God. The second temple to be built on the site by King Herod was destroyed by the Romans in 70 CE. The Wailing Wall is so called on account of the sorrowful prayers said there, mourning the loss of the temple.

Summary

You should now be able to describe and explain places of worship as a form of religious architecture.

2.5   Graveyards, statues and monuments

The afterlife

What happens after death is important to all religions. Followers of all six religions believe that death is not the end of life, but have different ideas about the form that survival after death takes. These different views about the afterlife are often conveyed by the religious architecture at burial sites, or memorials erected to the dead.

Religious architecture of graveyards

Graveyards are places where people are buried. The important features of religious architecture in graveyards include gravestones, edifices and statues.

Gravestones

Gravestones give a few details about the person buried in the grave. The design is often linked to the religion of the person buried there. For example, many Christian gravestones are in the shape of a cross and Jewish ones have the Star of David on them. In Islam, it is the rule that graves are raised between 4 and 12 inches from the ground. This is to prevent anyone from sitting or walking on the grave, which is strictly forbidden. Muslim gravestones are often very simple because it is thought the money would be better spent on helping the poor. Some gravestones in Jewish or Christian graveyards are more elaborate, relatives believing that this shows respect and honour to those who have died.

Edifices

Sometimes it is not thought sufficient to mark a person's grave with a simple gravestone, and huge **edifices** are built over them instead to show how important the person was in life.

Objectives

Investigate the significance of the architecture of graveyards, statues and monuments.

A   *A Jewish graveyard*

Key terms

Edifice: large, imposing building, often dedicated to some person/event.

Monument: often a large statue which is set up in commemoration of a person(s) or event.

Activity

Visit a local graveyard. See what you can find out about the religious beliefs of the people buried there by looking at the religious architecture.

Religious architecture of statues

Sometimes there are statues in a graveyard or on an individual grave to express a religious belief. The weeping angel in photograph **C** is intended to show sorrow at the loss of a loved one, but also the belief in an afterlife in heaven with the angels.

Statues are also found within Buddhist, Christian and Hindu places of worship. A statue of the Buddha is found in most Buddhist temples and shrines, usually showing the Buddha sitting cross legged in meditation.

B   *Edifices over graves in a graveyard*

The Buddha is placed higher than the worshippers to show the honour due to him. Roman Catholic (Christian) churches will probably contain statues of various saints, and always one of the Virgin Mary because she is the mother of Jesus and acts as an intermediary between God and believers. Hindu temples have statues of the gods or goddesses to whom the temple is dedicated.

Statues are not found in Islam, Judaism or Sikhism as it is felt that this could give the impression that it is the image that is being worshipped.

Religious architecture of monuments

Religious architecture may sometimes be in the form of **monuments**, erected at a place associated with a person important to the religion or a place of importance to its history.

One example of a religious monument is the Three Pillars at Mina, which are important to Muslims during pilgrimage (hajj). These three white stone pillars are at the three sites where the devil made three failed attempts to persuade Abraham not to sacrifice his son Ishmael to Allah. On the tenth day of pilgrimage, Muslims throw stones at these pillars to represent throwing the devil out of their lives.

   Statue of a weeping angel on a grave

Research activity

Using the internet and/or a library, research the attitude towards the use of statues in the places of worship of the religion(s) you are studying. Write an explanation of their use.

Extension activity

Using the internet and/or a library, find an example of a monument that is important to the religion(s) you are studying.

Discussion activity

With a partner, look at the photograph of the Jewish Holocaust Memorial. Discuss how it makes you feel and what you think the design of the monument is trying to say. Record your findings.

D   Jewish Holocaust Monument in Berlin

AQA   Examiner's tip

Make sure that you understand the specific ways in which the religion(s) you are studying uses graveyards for the dead.

Summary

You should now be able to describe and explain graveyards, statues and monuments as a form of religious architecture.

2.6 St Michael's Cathedral, Coventry – a case study

How was Coventry Cathedral produced?

In 1940, the medieval cathedral of St Michael's, Coventry was destroyed in a bombing raid. The next day, a cross was made from three huge medieval nails found in the ruins, and placed on what remained of the altar. It was decided to build a new cathedral. The cross of nails became a symbol that the new cathedral was to convey the spiritual message of reconciliation.

The new cathedral took seven years to build and was consecrated in 1962. It is faced with rose-red local sandstone, and the exterior and interior walls are very plain.

Inspiration

The spiritual experience the architect Sir Basil Spence had when he viewed the ruins of the old cathedral was the inspiration for his design of the new cathedral. He believed that, by building the new cathedral next to the ruins of the old cathedral and joining them together, he could express the Christian teaching of good triumphing over suffering through sacrifice. The ruined cathedral would represent sacrifice and the new cathedral would represent the triumph over death achieved through Christ's resurrection.

Revelation

The design of the whole building conveys the Christian message of suffering overcome through Christ's sacrifice. This message is revealed throughout many aspects of the exterior and interior of the Cathedral.

Devotion

The cathedral is a place of Christian worship and there are daily services. The instruction to the architect was that the central feature of the design must be the altar, as that would be the focus of the worship in the cathedral.

The very act of rebuilding the cathedral was also regarded as an act of devotion and donations of money and gifts for the cathedral came from all over the world. The font was made out of a boulder from the hillside above Bethlehem and, therefore, provides a link with the town in which Jesus was born.

links

Look back to pages 16–17 to remind yourself of the Christian teaching about the resurrection.

links

Look back to pages 34–35 to remind yourself of how religious architecture is produced.

A St. Michael's Cathedral, Coventry

Activity

1. a List the features you can see in the photograph of the cathedral and what you think they represent.
   b Check your list against the explanations given in 'Symbolism of the external features'.

AQA Examiner's tip

You need to be able to discuss at least one piece of religious architecture for the examination.

■ The symbolism of the cathedral

The symbolism of both the external and internal features is important in conveying the cathedral's message.

Symbolism of the external features

The spire of the cathedral represents a 'finger' pointing the way to heaven. It is a reminder to people that the way is open to God through worship of Jesus Christ.

On the wall near the entrance is Sir Jacob Epstein's bronze sculpture 'Saint Michael and the Devil', inspired by the account in the Book of Revelation (New Testament), of the Angel Michael conquering the devil. It reminds people that they can triumph over sin.

People enter the cathedral through a clear glass screen with etched images of saints and angels, which appear to be flying in and out of the cathedral. The screen is intended to provide the link between the old and new cathedrals. When in the new cathedral, the old cathedral is visible through the screen and vice versa.

Symbolism of the internal features

The font is near the door to symbolise that it is through baptism that people become members of the Christian faith.

The focal point of the cathedral is the altar, because it is here that the most important act of worship, Holy Communion, takes place. Behind, is a huge tapestry designed by Graham Sutherland, with symbols linked to Jesus and his teaching. For example, the four Gospel writers of the New Testament are represented by the symbols associated with them.

B *The font at Coventry Cathedral*

C *The High altar of Coventry Cathedral*

Summary

You should now be able to discuss the significance of a piece of religious architecture.

Religious architecture for private use

Sometimes people decide to have a place of worship for their private use – a place where they can worship alone or with their family. For example, someone living in a country where there are few members of their religion, or where they are not allowed to practise their religion as they would wish, might build or convert a building for private worship. Rich landowners sometimes build chapels so that they, their family and workers can worship together without having to go to a public place of worship. For example, the Queen has the Chapel of All Saints at Windsor for personal worship and privacy.

Occasionally, people become hermits and withdraw from everyday life to devote time to thinking about their faith on their own. They sometimes build a place of worship for their personal use. St Francis of Assisi (1181–1226) lived for several years as a hermit, and rebuilt a ruined chapel in the woods.

Religious architecture for personal use

B   *Buddhist temples are built for personal meditation*

A   *The Maisel synagogue in Prague, was built for the personal worship of the rich Maisel family*

🔗 links

Look back to pages 36–37 to remind yourself about religious architecture for public places of worship.

Look back to pages 40–41 to read about Coventry Cathedral – a public place of worship.

🔗 links

Look back to page 37 to remind yourself of the purpose of a stupa.

Look back to pages 12–13 to remind yourself of what is an icon.

The main purpose of Buddhist temples is to provide a place for personal meditation and offerings to the Buddha because individual devotion is so important to Buddhism. There is a Buddhist shrine containing a statue or image of the Buddha to help the worshipper remember the Buddha's teachings and the potential of everyone to attain enlightenment. There is a vase or tray of flowers to symbolise the impermanence of all living things. There are also miniature stupa and extract(s) from Buddhist texts that can be referred to as a reminder of Buddhist teaching.

Shrines within the home

C   *A Hindu home shrine*

Some people like to worship in the privacy of their own homes and a shrine may help with this. Shrines have different purposes according to the religion practised.

- Orthodox Christians have a shrine containing icons at which they pray daily.
- Hindu homes have a shrine with statues or pictures of the gods at which the daily worship (puja) is performed.
- Buddhist homes often have a miniature stupa, either to represent the Buddha's relics or to contain family relics.

Muslims do not require a structure for private worship. Instead, they need to face in the direction of the Ka'bah in Mecca, using something appropriate to show them the correct direction. Muslims usually kneel on a prayer mat to ensure that the place of prayer is clean and shows proper respect to Allah.

Activity

Write an explanation of how religious architecture may be used for personal and/or private use, giving specific examples.

Extension activity

Using the internet and/or a library, find examples of places of personal worship linked to the religion(s) you are studying.

Summary

You should now be able to explain how religious architecture is used in personal and/or private worship.

The intended impact

As with religious art, religious architecture is intended to make people think about God, religious truth or about the teachings of the religion. It is hoped that the architecture will help people to understand the religious message it was intended to convey. Very often places of worship will be found on hills, dominating the surrounding area to show the importance of God or the religion to the community.

Objectives

Investigate the impact of religious architecture on believers and non-believers.

AQA Examiner's tip

Remember to think about the influence of spirituality on believers and non-believers.

A *A place of worship will often dominate the area*

The impact of religious architecture on believers may be different from the impact on non-believers because of the different understanding they have about the message conveyed by the structure.

The impact of religious architecture on believers

A place specially designed for worship can be very valuable to individuals because going there can help them to focus on their faith. For example, Buddhist temples are designed as places of calm to help the worshippers meditate. Attending a place of worship is also a way of showing commitment to the faith.

Looking at the religious architecture reminds believers of the teaching of the religion, and this can strengthen their beliefs. It may enable them to make a spiritual response and aid devotion. The religious architecture provides an atmosphere that is right for prayer and meditation and an appropriate place in which to seek answers to the meaning of life. By attending a beautiful place of worship, the believer may feel closer to God or, in the case of Buddhists, closer to enlightenment.

B *Places of worship are often built on hills*

Research activity

Using the internet and/or a library, find out about the architecture of new places of worship in Britain. Write a brief account about the architecture of one of these places.

The impact of religious architecture on non-believers

The design of the exterior of the place of worship will probably make it identifiable as a place of worship even to non-believers. This may make them treat the place with more respect, even if they have no religious beliefs of their own. The beauty of the building may also invoke a spiritual response even if not a religious one. Sometimes entering a huge structure built to the glory of God can make people feel that there is a power controlling everything.

Religious architecture can also have a negative effect on non-believers and make them angry. Some people who are anti-religion, or have a prejudice against a specific religion, might decide to damage the building or deface it with graffiti.

Controversial religious architecture

Sometimes religious architecture can cause an outcry from both believers and non-believers – often about the money being spent on either the construction of a new building or the repairs to an existing building. People are divided on how much money should be spent on religious architecture. Many argue that it is wrong to spend large sums of money on places of worship or monuments because the money could be used for charity work instead. They might argue that religion advocates concern for others rather than buildings and that religion, in itself, is less important in the modern world.

C   *Many people objected to the spending of $40m on a new Hindu temple in Toronto*

Other religious believers agree that it is right to help the less fortunate, but it is also important to show devotion to God through religious architecture. Non-believers may support the money spent on religious architecture as it is maintaining the country's heritage and, even though they do not worship themselves, do not object to others who do having special places in which to worship.

2.9 What does religious architecture tell us about God, belief and the architect?

What does religious architecture tell us about God?

Religious architecture helps to show people the importance of God to the religion, and the religion's teaching about God. Structures with spires pointing towards heaven act as reminders that God is above everyone. The beauty of the building stresses the majesty of God. A large place of worship emphasises the vastness of God and that he is omnipotent. In very large places of worship, people are reminded how small humans are in comparison to God. A dome over the building teaches that God is over everything, knows everything and is everywhere.

A *The beauty and grandeur of a place of worship expresses attributes of God*

Like a larger building, a small intimate place of worship can show that God may be outside time and space and beyond human understanding, but it also shows that God can come close and be present in the world. Such a place might encourage an individual to talk directly to God.

What does religious architecture tell us about belief?

The form of worship in a particular religion shapes the design of the building. Christian churches are often built in the shape of a cross, and the prayer hall in a mosque will show the direction of prayer. Buddhists do not believe in God, so there is no reference to God in the design of Buddhist temples, but in many temples the size of the Buddha incorporated into the design of the building emphasises his importance to the faith.

In Christianity, there are many different denominations with different ideas about how worship should be performed. The different denominations, therefore, require different features within their buildings. For example, there is a font for baptising babies in Anglican, Catholic and Orthodox churches, but in the Baptist Church adults are baptised, so there is a pool called a baptistery. The service of Holy Communion may require an altar or a table according to what Christians believe about the meaning of Jesus' teaching at the Last Supper.

B *Many Buddhist temples are dominated by a statue of the Buddha*

Therefore, the design of the building indicates what is important to the particular religion within its religious teachings, which also dictate what cannot be included in the design.

What does religious architecture tell us about the architect?

What religious architecture tells us about the architect depends on the reasons for the construction of the building or structure. The architect may have designed the building to match the brief of the client. For example, Sir Basil Spence was employed to build Coventry Cathedral and, for his design to be successful, he needed to ensure that it matched the needs of the Christians who were going to worship there. It was this understanding of the Christian faith that inspired him to create a place of worship that underlined the beliefs and teachings of the faith. To really understand the mind of the architect, it is probably necessary to know something about the inspiration that led to the design of the piece of religious architecture.

Research activity

Choose a place of worship. Using the internet and/or a library, find out what is needed in the building for worship in the religion chosen. Write an account of what the religious architecture tells people about the religious beliefs of the religion.

C *Some Christians are baptised in a pool*

∞links

Look back to page 40 to remind yourself of the influences that led to Sir Basil Spence's design for Coventry Cathedral.

Activities

1. Explain what religious architecture can tell us about God. Give some examples from the religion you are studying.
2. Explain what religious architecture can tell us about belief. Give some examples from the religion you are studying.
3. Explain what religious architecture can tell us about the architect. Give some examples from the religion you are studying.

Summary

You should now be able to explain what religious architecture tells us about God, belief and the architect.

2.10 The symbolic nature of religious architecture and its place in the modern world

The symbolic nature of religious architecture

The symbolism of the architecture may encourage people to think about some aspect of life or faith, and is intended to convey aspects of the religion's teaching. It may serve as a reminder of the importance of individuals and events to the religion. Below are some examples of the symbolic nature of religious architecture.

Buddhism

The shape of the stupa, or temple, represents the five elements – fire, air, earth, water and wisdom. The square base is the earth, and the dome represents water. The stone fence around the base represents fire, while the pyramid shape above links to air. The pinnacle on the top is symbolic of the enlightenment that Buddhists are seeking.

Objectives

Investigate the symbolic nature of religious architecture.

Investigate the place of religious architecture as a form of spirituality in the modern world.

links

Look back to pages 36–39 to remind yourself of the symbolism found in places of worship and shrines.

A A Buddhist stupa

B Orthodox Churches have a dome that represents heaven

Christianity

Orthodox churches have a dome that represents heaven, and reminds people that to gain God's blessing it is necessary to accept salvation through Christ. It is circular to represent the eternity of God. Churches built in the shape of a cross remind people that Jesus died on the cross to save them from sin.

Hinduism

Each Hindu temple (mandir) is dedicated to a particular god or goddess. The building itself represents the nature of the universe and is regarded as the home of the god to whom it is dedicated. As a result, the temple is not only a place of worship but an object of worship in itself.

Islam

The mosque will have a tall tower called a minaret, from which the call to prayer (adhan) is given five times a day, and a dome as a reminder of the universe and the great love of Allah. The dome is often green because this is regarded as the colour of nature in Islam and is a reminder of the beauty of Allah's creation.

Judaism

The most important feature inside the synagogue is the Ark where the Torah is kept. The Ark is a cupboard with either doors or curtains that are only opened to take out the scrolls needed for worship. It is named after the Ark of the Covenant, which held the Ten Commandments in Moses's time, and is set in the wall facing Jerusalem where the temple stood.

Sikhism

A Sikh gurdwara is recognisable by the Sikh flag with the Sikh emblem (the nishan sahib) that is erected outside. The nishan sahib symbolises all that Sikhs believe about God. The two outer crossed swords symbolise God's spiritual power. The ring of steel represents the unity of God and the double-edged sword in the centre, God's concern for truth and justice.

 The Sikh flag

■ The place of religious architecture in the modern world

Religious buildings are not usually just places of worship. Many are also used for other activities, such as holding meetings to discuss issues that are important to the community as a whole. Many activities in a religious building may also be attended by non-believers. These activities include:

- community meetings
- social gatherings
- rites of passage – ceremonies, marriages, funerals
- leisure and keep-fit activities, such as drama groups and dance classes
- educational activities, such as the teaching of Hebrew, Arabic or confirmation classes
- those involving young people, such as playgroups, Brownies, Scouts and youth clubs.

Activities

1. Explain the importance of symbolism to religious architecture, supporting your answer with examples.
2. 'Places of worship are still important in the modern world.' Do you agree? Give reasons for your answer, showing that you have thought about more than one point of view.

Summary

You should now be able to discuss the symbolic nature of religious architecture, and the place of religious architecture as a form of spirituality in the modern world.

Research activity ⚲

Using the internet and/or a library, find out more details of **one** religion's beliefs and form of worship. Find out and write a description of how the beliefs and worship have affected the symbolism of the architecture of the religion's place of worship.

∞ links

Look back to page 45 to remind yourself of possible views for and against building places of worship in the modern world.

Discussion activity ∎∎∎

With a partner, in a small group or as a whole class, discuss the following statement: 'Religious buildings should only be used for worship.' Do you agree? Give reasons for your answer, showing that you have thought about more than one point of view.

AQA   *Examiner's tip*

Remember, you should always support your answers with examples from the religion(s) you have studied.

2

AQA *Examiner's tip*

Remember, you may refer to one or more than one religion/denomination in this section of the examination.

Religion and art – summary

For the examination you should now be able to:

- ✓ describe and explain what is meant by 'spirituality'
- ✓ describe and explain what is meant by 'religious architecture'
- ✓ describe and explain different types of religious architecture including places of worship, graveyard architecture, edifices, monuments and statues
- ✓ describe and explain how and why religions use architecture
- ✓ explain how religious architecture is used in worship (personal and/or private)
- ✓ explain the impact of religious architecture on those looking on – believers and non-believers
- ✓ explain what religious architecture tells us about God, belief and the architect
- ✓ explain the symbolic nature of this form of spirituality
- ✓ evaluate the place of religious architecture as a form of spirituality in the modern world.

Sample answer

1 Write an answer to the following examination question:

'God does not need a place of worship.' Do you agree? Give reasons for your answer, showing that you have thought about more than one point of view. Refer to religious arguments in your answer. *(6 marks)*

2 Read the sample answer below:

Buddhists would agree with this statement as they don't believe in God. Other religions are undecided. Some people say we should worship at home as God knows what we are saying wherever we are. Muhammad said, 'The earth has been made for me and for my followers as a masjid and a place for purification; therefore, any one of my followers can pray whenever the time of prayer is due.' God might not need the

place of worship, but the followers do as they can meet together in a place special to them.

God might like a place of worship as it shows the people believe in him and it would be nice for him to feel close to them in a special place. Hindus believe the temple is the home of the gods, so they must visit them there like family.

3 With a partner, discuss the sample answer. Do you think that there are other things that the student could have included in the answer?

4 What mark would you give this answer out of 6? (Look at the mark scheme in the Introduction on page 7 (AO2) before you attempt this.) What are the reasons for the mark you have given?

AQA Examination-style questions

1 Look at the photograph and answer the following questions.

(a) Give **two** types of religious architecture.   (*2 marks*)

The word 'give' indicates that you can just write down two types of religious architecture, without any further detail.

(b) Explain briefly three different kinds of religious architecture.   (*3 marks*)

Explain **three** different kinds of religious architecture for a maximum of 1 mark each.

(c) 'Religious architecture is very effective at expressing a spiritual message.'
What do you think? Explain your opinion.   (*3 marks*)

When you are asked this type of question, try to write about 6 lines in response.

(d) Explain, using examples, the impact of religious art on believers and non-believers.   (*4 marks*)

Make sure that you consider both believers **and** non-believers.

(e) 'We should not spend money on places of worship.' Do you agree?
Give reasons for your answer, showing that you have thought about more
than one point of view. Refer to religious arguments in your answer.   (*6 marks*)

Remember that when you are given a statement and asked 'do you agree?' you must show what you think and the reasons why other people might take a different view. If your answer is one-sided, you can only achieve a maximum of 4 marks. If you make no comment about religious belief or practice, you will achieve no more than 3 marks.

3.1 What is literature?

Defining literature

'Literature' is a term used to describe written material that is thought to have artistic merit. Broadly speaking, 'literature' is used today to describe the use of words from creative writing to more technical or scientific works, but the term usually refers to works of the creative imagination that include:

■ poetry – composition in verse or language that deliberately has a pattern

■ prose – ordinary writing that can be fiction or non-fiction, but not verse:

  – fiction – writing based on imagination rather than fact

  – non-fiction – writing that is factual, for example biographies, textbooks or commentaries on other writings

■ drama – a dramatic work intended for performance by actors.

The influences on literature

There are many reasons why people choose to write a piece of literature other than the desire to become rich and famous. J.K. Rowling said, 'I was convinced that the only thing I wanted to do, ever, was to write novels.' Many writers would agree with her and say that writing was the only thing that they wanted to do, and they felt driven to do it.

Other writers may be influenced by a message that they want to share with society, or the desire to change things that they think are wrong. Charles Dickens (1812–70) was always interested in social reform. He hoped that by describing the hardship, cruelty and poverty of the poor in Victorian England, the life of the poor would improve. Dickens showed in his novels how brutal and unfeeling the treatment of the poor was by setting scenes in places such as the workhouse in *Oliver Twist* (1837–8), or the debtor's prison in *Little Dorrit* (1855–7). Other authors might want to make political changes. The writing of Russian author, Alexander Solschenizyn (1918–2008) intended to make the world aware of faults in the political system in the Soviet Union (Russia) in the 1950s.

A The literary works of William Shakespeare are the best known in the world

The internal economy of Dothebys Hall

B Dickens tried to bring about social reform through his writing, such as an improvement in education

Case study

Cathy Come Home

The play *Cathy Come Home* was shown on BBC television in 1966. The drama showed the effect of being homeless upon the family. The watching public was shocked by how a young family could be separated by social services, and the children taken into care because they had become homeless through no fault of their own. People demanded action and the result was the founding of the housing action charity, Shelter.

The influence of spirituality on literature

As with art and architecture, another major influence on literature is spirituality. Writers experience moments when they have become aware in some way of the underlying truths of the world. This results in the writer feeling the need to communicate this revelation to others; or to express in words what they have felt. Poetry is often the result of such spiritual feelings. For example, the writer could feel moved to communicate some aspect of the beauty of nature that they have experienced. Wordsworth wrote a famous poem describing how he felt when he saw a 'host of golden daffodils' and how thinking about them still gave him pleasure long after he returned home.

Many writers seek to explore what is meant by spirituality and spiritual experiences in their writing. The supernatural and the conflict between good and evil are familiar themes in many literary works. The novel *Dracula* is very much about spiritual matters such as love, friendship, courage, the afterlife, as well as the theme of good against evil.

C *The poet William Wordsworth had a spiritual experience when he saw a bank of daffodils*

AQA **Examiner's tip**

Make sure that you understand the relationship between spirituality and literature because you may be asked to discuss it in the examination.

D *The story of* Dracula *is concerned with spiritual matters such as the boundary between life and death*

∞ links

Look back to pages 8–9 to remind yourself of what is meant by spirituality.

Activities

1. Explain what is meant by 'literature'.
2. Explain how spirituality influences literature.

Summary

You should now be able to explain what is meant by literature and the influence of spirituality on literature.

wrath;
do not fret—it leads only to evil.
⁹For evil men will be cut off,
but those who hope in the Lord will
inherit the land.

¹⁰A little while, and the wicked will be no
more;

he makes his steps firm;
²⁴though he stumble, he will not fall,
for the Lord upholds him with his
hand.

²⁵I was young and now I am old,
yet I have never seen the righteous
forsaken

Consider the blameless, observe the
upright;
there is a future for the man of peace.
But all sinners will be destroyed;
the future of the wicked will be cut off.

The salvation of the righteous comes
from the Lord;

who seek my life set their traps,
those who would harm me talk of my
ruin;
all day long they plot deception.

¹³I am like a deaf man, who cannot hear,
like a mute, who cannot open his
mouth;
¹⁴I have become like

3.2   What is religious literature?

■ What is religious literature?

Religious **literature** is writing that deals with religious themes or includes a religious view of the world – a particular understanding of the meaning of life, the importance of human beings in the world and the origins of the world itself. This is usually specific to the religion to which the writing belongs and is based on religious beliefs and/or science. Such literature usually contains what the believer or religion claims to be true about the existence of God, the origin of the universe and/or the purpose and meaning of life. There are many types of religious literature, including:

- holy books
- non-fiction such as writings about the meaning of the holy books
- works of fiction with a religious theme
- drama with a religious theme
- religious poetry.

A The Lion, the Witch and the Wardrobe *has been adapted for film and TV and carries a spiritual message*

Objectives

Understand what is meant by religious literature.

Explore the contribution of religious literature to spirituality.

Key terms

Literature: range of writings, e.g. stories, scripture, diaries or poems.

AQA Examiner's tip

In your examination answers, you may refer to one religion or a combination of any of the specified religions. The specified religions are Buddhism, Christianity, Hinduism, Islam, Judaism or Sikhism.

∞ links

See pages 58–61 to examine types of religious literature in more detail.

■ Spirituality through religious literature

Some literature may cause people to respond spiritually to the writing because of the beauty of the words, or the effects of the story as it unfolds. In religious literature, writers examine spiritual questions related to aspects of religious belief, such as whether or not God exists, or how to live a life that achieves reward in the afterlife. The writers are sharing their experience and findings with others in the hope that they will also find answers to religious or spiritual questions.

∞ links

Look back to pages 8–9 to remind yourself of what is meant by spirituality.

B   *'The plane developed engine trouble'*

Drama in the Air

A doctor, a lawyer, a little boy and a priest were out for a Sunday afternoon flight on a small private plane. Suddenly, the plane developed engine trouble. In spite of the best efforts of the pilot the plane started to go down. Finally the pilot grabbed a parachute, yelled to the passengers that they had better jump, and bailed out.

Unfortunately there were only three parachutes remaining.

The doctor grabbed one and said 'I'm a doctor, I save lives, so I must live,' and jumped out.

The lawyer then said, 'I'm a lawyer and lawyers are the smartest people in the world, I deserve to live!' He grabbed a parachute and jumped.

The priest looked at the little boy and said, 'My son, I've lived a long and full life. You are young and have your whole life ahead of you. Take the last parachute and live in peace.'

The little boy handed the parachute back to the priest and said, 'Not to worry, Father. The "smartest man in the world" just took off with my back pack.'

L. M. Myers

Discussion activity 👥

In a group, read L. M. Myers Drama in the Air below and discuss the spiritual message that the story is teaching. Record your findings.

Activities

1   Explain what is meant by 'religious literature'.

2   Explain the spiritual influence of religious literature on people.

Extension activities

1   Why is *The Lion, the Witch and the Wardrobe* considered to be religious literature?

2   Find your own examples of religious literature.

Summary

You should now be able to explain what is meant by religious literature and the contribution of literature to spirituality.

wrath;
do not fret—it leads only to evil.
⁸For evil men will be cut off,
but those who hope in the LORD will
inherit the land.

¹⁰A little while, and the wicked will be no
more;

he makes his steps firm;
²⁴though he stumble, he will not fall,
for the LORD upholds him with his
hand.

²⁵I was young and now I am old,
yet I have never seen the righteous
forsaken

's way.
upright;
there is a future for the man of peace.
but all sinners will be destroyed;
the future of the wicked will be cut off.

the salvation of the righteous comes
from the LORD;
stronghold in time of trouble

those who would harm me talk of my
ruin;
all day long they plot deception.

¹³I am like a deaf man, who cannot hear,
like a mute, who cannot open his
mouth;
¹⁴I have become like

3.3   The production of religious literature

▮ How is religious literature produced?

Religious literature is produced for many of the reasons shared with art and architecture. The main difference is that writers use words to put forward their ideas. The number of words used to express religious ideas can vary from poems of a few lines to the estimated 774,746 words in the Christian Bible.

Revelation

Holy books are examples of revelation, although the way in which they are revealed may vary from religion to religion. The writers are believed to have received revelations directly from God/Allah, as in the case of the Muslim Qur'an, or through God inspiring the writers to communicate his message using their own words, as in the case of the Sikh Guru Granth Sahib.

Other writers recorded revelations that they received through a religious experience to help believers deepen their understanding of the holy books and teachings of a religion. For example, Guru Gobind Singh's (1666–1708) writings, which help to guide Sikhs, are collected together in Dasm Granth, meaning *Book of the Tenth Emperor*. In 1563, John Foxe had a vision that led him to record accounts of the deaths of the Protestant martyrs (people who suffer or die for their beliefs) during Mary Tudor's reign, as a revelation to others of how faith can triumph over suffering.

Buddhists are seeking enlightenment; understanding of how to escape the suffering of the cycle of birth and death and achieve happiness. Much of their religious literature is based on the enlightenment that other Buddhists have achieved, especially the revelations of the Buddha.

Inspiration

Religious literature may be inspired by other literature or experiences. For example, the holy books may inspire writers to comment on specific religious passages or writings. Such commentaries are written to help people study these writings.

The life of the founder of the religion or some other leading figure within the religion may inspire a biography or play about their life and work. For example, there have been many biographies of the life of the prophet Muhammad. Austrian Heinrich Harrer was deeply affected by his time with the Dalai Lama in Tibet and recorded his experiences in his book *Seven Years in Tibet*. This, in turn, inspired director Jean-Jacques Annaud to make his adventures into a film of the same name.

∞ links

Look back to page 11 and pages 34–35 to remind yourself of how religious art and architecture are produced.

A   *Revelations of the Buddha have been written down*

The writer's religious beliefs may also be a source of inspiration and form an underlying theme for his or her fictional writing. For example, the Italian writer Dante Alighieri wrote the *Divine Comedy* (1308–21). This vision of the Christian afterlife, in turn, inspired the writings of others, such as T.S. Eliot's poem *The Hollow Man* (1925).

B   Torture of the Fiery Rain: *an engraving from Dante's* Divine Comedy

Discussion activity

Look at the photograph of the engraving from Dante's *Divine Comedy*. The book describes the tortures of hell as well as the rewards of heaven. What effect do you think such ideas would have on other people reading his work? Record your findings.

Activity

Write an explanation of how religious literature is the result of revelation, inspiration or devotion. Support your answer with examples.

Extension activity

Find out more about the Oberammergau passion plays.

The Oberammergau passion plays

When an outbreak of plague swept through Europe, the people of Oberammergau, Austria vowed that if their village was spared, they would perform a play based on the suffering, death and resurrection of Jesus Christ. In 1634, they kept their promise and over the next 376 years have continued to perform the play every 10 years as an act of devotion and thanks to God.

C   The Oberammergau plays are performed as acts of devotion

Case study

Devotion

Religious literature is often written as an act of devotion. Many poems are intended to show the writer's love of God or of a religious figure. In the Christian and Jewish religions, The Book of Psalms contains poems in praise of God.

Sometimes plays are performed as an act of devotion or to teach others how and why they could get closer to God.

Summary

You should now know, and be able to explain, how religious literature is produced.

wrath;
do not fret—it leads only to evil.
⁹For evil men will be cut off,
but those who hope in the LORD will
inherit the land.

¹⁰A little while, and the wicked will be no
more;

he makes his steps firm;
²⁴though he stumble, he will not fall,
for the LORD upholds him with his
hand.

²⁵I was young and now I am old,
yet I have never seen the righteous
forsaken

Consider the blameless, observe the
upright;
there is a future for the man of peace.
that all sinners will be destroyed;
the future of the wicked will be cut off.
The salvation of the righteous comes
from the LORD;
stronghold in time of trouble

my life set their traps,
those who would harm me talk of my
ruin;
all day long they plot deception.

¹³I am like a deaf man, who cannot hear,
like a mute, who cannot open his
mouth;
¹⁴I have become like a

3.4 Holy books and books of teachings

◼ Holy books

Religious belief depends on faith. The most important authority, which helps people to trust God and their religion, is the holy book of a religion, supported by other books of teachings.

Religious believers do not agree about the authority of their holy book as the Word of God. Fundamentalists regard these holy books as the direct Word of God, containing no errors as the writers recorded God's revelations, word for word. To them, every word of the scripture is the literal truth. Others accept a non-literal view, believing that the writers did not record God's message word for word, but interpreted it and brought their own personalities and styles to the writing.

Buddhism

The Tripitaka is not given divine authority because Buddhists do not believe in God. It is a collection of texts divided into the Word of the Buddha (sutta); the rules of discipline for monastic life (vinaya); and commentaries on teachings (abhidhamma).

Christianity

The Bible is not one but 66 books written over many centuries, divided into two main sections called the Old and New Testaments. Christians agree that the Bible is in some way the Word of God, but do not agree that it is the only source of knowledge about God. For example, the Roman Catholic Church accepts an oral tradition passed down from Jesus through the Church as another source of knowledge about God.

Hinduism

There are many holy books in Hinduism. The shruti is the oldest and most sacred, and contains revelations from God to holy men. These include four collections called the Vedas, considered holy by all Hindus. They explain how religious life and duty should be carried out.

Islam

The Qur'an is the Muslim holy book, described as a 'living miracle' because it is believed to be the direct Word of Allah for all people and all times, given in a revelation to the prophet Muhammad to recite.

Judaism

The Tenakh is the Jewish holy book. The most important part is the Torah: the Five Books of Moses that contain the complete Jewish law. The Tenakh also contains the eight books of the Prophets and the 11 books of Writings, which include the Psalms of David.

A *A Buddhist prayer book*

B *Torah scrolls*

Sikhism

The Guru Granth Sahib is the Sikh holy book and is respected as a living teacher – a guru. It contains the teachings of the first five Sikh Gurus, as well as sections from Hindu and Muslim teachings, collected by Guru Arjan and Guru Gobind Singh.

C   *The Guru Granth Sahib is respected as a living teacher*

Research activity

1   Choose **one** holy book from the religions discussed and, using the internet and/or a library, find out more about it. Write a description of the holy book as a work of religious literature.

Discussion activity

As a whole class, discuss whether you think people learn more or less about God through holy books. Record your findings.

Research activity

2   In a small group, research the books of religious teaching from **one** of the six religions studied. Present your findings to the class using presentation software.

Books of religious teachings

Each religion has additional teachings from God or leading teachers to help people understand their holy book or how to live according to its teachings. Below are some examples:

Buddhism

Dhamma contains the teachings of the Buddha about the universal truth and universal law.

Christianity

The Apocrypha is a collection of books containing moral and uplifting stories. Catholics include the Apocrypha in the Old Testament. Some Christians consider that they are not equal to the other books of the Bible and do not include them in it.

Hinduism

The smriti is a collection of human interpretations of God's teachings and stories of the gods and goddesses.

Islam

Hadith is a collection of the sayings of Muhammad and is a major source of Islamic law.

Judaism

The Talmud is a commentary by Jewish religious teachers on how the law is to be followed.

Sikhism

The Dasm Granth is a collection of writings, mainly from Guru Gobind Singh.

D   *The Talmud is commentary by Jewish religious teachers.*

Summary

You should now be able to describe and discuss holy books and books of teachings as forms of religious literature.

Consider the blameless, ...
upright;
there is a future for the man of peace.
But all sinners will be destroyed;
the future of the wicked will be cut off.
The salvation of the righteous comes
from the LORD;
...stronghold in time of trouble

wrath;
do not fret—it leads only to evil.
For evil men will be cut off,
but those who hope in the LORD will
inherit the land.

A little while, and the wicked will be no
more;

he makes his steps firm;
though he stumble, he will not fall,
for the LORD upholds him with his
hand.

I was young and now I am old,
yet I have never seen the righteous
forsaken

those who would harm me talk of my
ruin;
all day long they plot deception.

I am like a deaf man, who cannot hear,
like a mute, who cannot open his
mouth;
I have become like...

3.6 'Diary of a Church Mouse' – a case study

A *Sir John Betjeman (1906–1984)*

How was the poem produced?

Sir John Betjeman (1906–1984) was a poet, broadcaster and journalist. He was a member of the Church of England and used his poetry to put forward his Christian beliefs. The poem 'Diary of a Church Mouse' was included in his collection of poems called *Poems in the Porch* (1954). The porch in the title of the book refers to the church porch where people meet after church services. The poem was broadcast on a Sunday evening in 1953. In the 1950s, Sunday was considered to be a day of worship by most people in Britain, and time was given by radio and television on Sundays for acts of worship and programmes with a Christian theme.

Inspiration

The poem was written to be read by Betjeman on radio. The BBC asked Betjeman to write a weekly diary of a church mouse for broadcast. He was inspired by this request and his own faith to write a humorous poem addressing issues related to falling church attendance.

Revelation

Betjeman had become aware of the decline in church attendance and people's struggle to believe. He felt that there was a clash between how the Church of England taught people to behave according to their faith and how they actually lived their lives. For example, he thought that many people were becoming selfish and greedy.

◼ The symbolism of the poem

At the beginning of Betjeman's poem, the mouse describes its lonely and hungry life in the church for most of the year. It is surprised that there is not even abundant food at the three major Christian festivals: Christmas, remembering Jesus's birth; Easter, the festival remembering Jesus rising from the dead; and Whitsun (Pentecost), the feast that celebrates the Holy Spirit coming to the Apostles.

Through the symbolism of the loneliness and meagre diet of the mouse, Betjeman is pointing out that the churches are empty, even at the most important festivals for Christians. The churches are empty at the times when they should be full and, yet, at the time of the lesser festival of Harvest, when thanks is given to God for the gifts of food, churches are full, and many of those who attend are not really believers. Betjeman uses the symbolism of 'other mice with pagan minds' and 'two field mice who have no desire to be baptised' to show that there are other reasons why some people attend church rather than religious belief. Even atheists attend the Harvest service, as represented by the 'unfriendly rat'.

Betjeman uses the references to other rodents to symbolise people who attend church services from the desire to be seen for social reasons rather than to worship God. Such people are hypocrites as they attend church pretending to have religious belief, but the fact that they attend church only for the Harvest festival demonstrates that they either have little faith or none at all. Such people want to be seen as Christian, but the fact that they are selfish and inconsiderate is demonstrated by their failure to help those in need, those 'who starve the whole year through'.

Betjeman ends the poem by explaining how a true believer should behave through the mouse's thoughts on human worship.

> ❝ *Christmas and Easter may be feasts*
> *For congregations and for priests,*
> *And so may Whitsun. All the same,*
> *They do not fill my meagre frame.* ❞
>
> From 'Diary of a Church Mouse'

> ❝ *A large and most unfriendly rat*
> *Comes in to see what we are at.*
> *He says he thinks there is no God*
> *And yet he comes… it's rather odd.* ❞
>
> From 'Diary of a Church Mouse'

> ❝ *For human beings only do*
> *What their religion tells them to.*
> *Within the human world I know*
> *They read the Bible every day*
> *And always, night and morning, pray,*
> *And just like me, the good church mouse,*
> *Worship each week in God's own house.* ❞
>
> From 'Diary of a Church Mouse'

Activity

Write a detailed explanation, with examples, of how the poem 'Diary of a Church Mouse', or another poem from the religion(s) you are studying, expresses religious teaching.

Summary

You should now have some ideas and skills that will help you to discuss a piece of religious literature.

wrath;
do not fret—it leads only to evil.
⁹For evil men will be cut off,
but those who hope in the LORD will
inherit the land.

¹⁰A little while, and the wicked will be no
more;

he makes his steps firm;
²⁴though he stumble, he will not fall,
for the LORD upholds him with his
hand.

²⁵I was young and now I am old,
yet I have never seen the righteous
forsaken

...upright;
...there is a future for the man of peace.
...all sinners will be destroyed;
...the future of the wicked will be cut off.

...the salvation of the righteous comes
from the LORD;
...stronghold in time of trouble

...those who would harm me talk of my
ruin;
all day long they plot deception.

¹³I am like a deaf man, who cannot hear,
like a mute, who cannot open his
mouth;
¹⁴I have become like...

3.7 How religious literature is used in worship

How religious literature is used in public worship

Religious literature is used to support public worship to teach the religion's message. This may be through readings from the religion's holy books that are later explained in sermons. In many religions, drama is used to teach or remind believers of some aspect of their faith. In Christianity, nativity plays are used to teach children why Christmas is celebrated. Hindus and Sikhs use drama during the festival of Diwali to teach or remind people of aspects of the religion(s). Annually in Iran, Muslims perform dramas that commemorate the martyrdom of Muslims at the battle of Karbala (680 CE).

∞ links

Look back to pages 58–61 to remind yourself of the different types of literature.

Objectives

Investigate how religious literature is used in public and private worship.

∞ links

Look back to page 20 to be sure that you understand the difference between public and private worship.

Look back to pages 58–59 to remind yourself of the holy books of the religion(s) you are studying.

A *Martyrdom at the battle of Karbala is re-enacted in Iran*

Research activity

Using the internet and/or a library, find out how literature is used in the religion(s) you are studying. Write an explanation of how literature is used in the public worship of the religion(s) you have researched.

Religious literature for personal and/or private use

Religious literature not only has a central role in public worship, but is very important to the personal and private worship of believers. Famous preachers' sermons are available for believers to read for themselves, and possibly discuss with other believers. Muslims often have the last sermon of Muhammad on the walls of their homes as a constant reminder of what it means to be a Muslim. For Buddhists, the Buddha's sermons are a personal guide to follow to achieve nirvana.

A major support for personal and private worship is the religion's holy book, and most believers will try to read sections daily. For example, during Ramadan, which celebrates the first revelation of the Islamic scripture, Muslims are encouraged to read the whole Qur'an. Reading sections from the holy book is important to religious believers not only to help concentration during private prayer and meditation, but also as a guide to daily life. Sikhs will have sections from the Guru Granth Sahib in their homes for use during private prayer. Attached to the doorpost of a Jewish home is a small decorated box called a mezuzah, which contains the Shema as a constant reminder that Jews should love God and keep his rules. Hindus will read sections from their holy books. For example, by reading the Bhagavad Gita (The Song of the Lord) from the *Mahabharata*, they will be led to think about questions such as 'What is people's duty to God?' and 'What is their relationship with God?'

Many believers use not only their holy book in private worship but other religious literature as well. Most Christians have a prayer book to help private devotion. Some Catholics use a psalter to aid prayer. During the Seder meal held in each Jewish family's home at the beginning of Passover, the story of their deliverance is read from Haggadah, which contains the words used during the Passover meal.

B   *The doorposts of Jewish homes have mezuzahs*

Writing fictional literature, poetry and drama may be prompted by a personal need for the writer to express their feelings about God or their religion. However, reading religious fiction and poetry, as well as watching drama productions, gives people pleasure as a leisure activity as well as being used during acts of public and private worship.

Activity

Write an explanation of how religious literature may be used for public and/or private use. Remember to include examples in your answer.

Summary

You should now be able to explain how religious literature is used in public and/or private worship.

AQA   Examiner's tip

Make sure that you can give specific examples of the public and private use of religious literature to support your answers in the examination.

wrath;
do not fret—it leads only to evil.
⁹For evil men will be cut off,
but those who hope in the LORD will
inherit the land.

¹⁰A little while, and the wicked will be no
more;

he makes his steps firm;
²⁴though he stumble, he will not fall,
for the LORD upholds him with his
hand.

²⁵I was young and now I am old,
yet I have never seen the righteous
forsaken

Consider the blameless, observe the
upright;
there is a future for the man of peace.
But all sinners will be destroyed;
the future of the wicked will be cut off.

The salvation of the righteous comes
from the LORD;
stronghold in time of trouble

those who would harm me talk of my
ruin;
all day long they plot deception

¹³I am like a deaf man, who cannot hear,
like a mute, who cannot open his
mouth;
¹⁴I have become like

3.8 The impact of religious literature

■ The impact of religious literature on believers

Holy books and collections of teachings provide additional support to believers of the truth of their religion. For example, Muslims believe that no human could create words of such beauty as those of the Qur'an, and this is one reason for believing that the words are Allah's words. They believe that each word of the Qur'an must influence every aspect of their life.

Beliefs and teachings

God! There is no god but He, - the Living
The Self –Subsisting, Eternal
It is He who sent down
To thee (step by step) in truth the Book.

Qur'an 3:2–3

With the exception of Buddhism, the other religions all agree that the holy books are inspired in some way by God, as a guide to life. The teachings of the Buddha guide Buddhists towards enlightenment.

Religious literature from leading teachers helps to explain the religious texts and to bring greater understanding. Reading the lives of other religious believers may be an inspiration to follow or learn from their example.

Objectives

Investigate the impact of religious literature on believers and non-believers.

A *The beauty of the words of the Qur'an is evidence to Muslims that they are the words of Allah*

AQA Examiner's tip

Remember to think about the influence of spirituality on believers **and** non-believers.

Research activity 🔍

1 a Using the internet and/or a library, research how religious literature influenced one of the following believers and changed his/her life:
- Richard Gere (Buddhism)
- Gladys Aylward (Christianity)
- Ghandi (Hinduism)
- Khadija (Islam)
- Anne Frank (Judaism)
- Guru Gobind Singh (Sikhism)

   b How has the life/writings of your chosen believer influenced others?

   c Write an account of the impact of religious literature on the believer researched.

■ The impact of religious literature on non-believers

Religious believers think that the beauty of religious literature and the truth contained in it is sufficient to convert non-believers to the religion. There are many examples of non-believers who have converted through the power of religious literature. It may be a passage from a holy book, reading a poem or watching a play that has made them feel that there is a power greater than themselves. From this spiritual experience, they have felt the desire to seek answers to the questions raised in their minds and often they will seek to find the answers in the literature of the religion.

Religious literature can have the opposite effect and convince atheists that they are right in rejecting the existence of God. Many atheists argue that the existence of different holy books claiming to support the 'true' religion proves that they cannot all be right and that God does not exist; if he did, then he would send just one shared holy book.

■ Religious literature can be controversial

Sometimes religious literature is censored; either all or part of it is deleted so that it does not cause offence. This often leads to disputes between those banning the work, which they believe is contrary to their religious beliefs, and those who feel that they have the right to decide for themselves whether or not the work is blasphemous, offensive or contradicts the teachings of the religion. Here are three examples of banned religious literature:

- In the 16th century, Galileo's scientific writings, proving that the earth went round the sun, were suppressed by the Roman Catholic Church and Galileo was held under house arrest. This was because the Catholic Church feared Galileo's findings would undermine their religious teachings.

- In 2004, a Birmingham theatre cancelled the performance of the play *Behzti* (Dishonour) by playwright Gurpreet Kaur Bhatti. This was because the play depicted sexual abuse and murder in a gurdwara.

- Salman Rushdie's novel *The Satanic Verses* as detailed in the case study below.

The Satanic Verses

Case study

In 1988, the author Salman Rushdie wrote a novel called *The Satanic Verses*. There was an immediate worldwide Muslim outcry against the book, as it was felt that the author had insulted the prophet Muhammad and his wives, as well as Muslim religious leaders, within the story. The book was publically burned by Muslims and stores selling it were firebombed. The spiritual leader of Iran, Ayatollah Khomeini called the book 'blasphemous against Islam' and gave an instruction called a 'fatwah' that Muslims were to find and kill Rushdie. The author lived in hiding for almost 10 years. This led to controversy within the Muslim community, and between Muslims and non-Muslims. Many Muslims did not agree with the fatwah and many non-Muslims did not agree with censorship of the book.

Discussion activity 👤👤👤

Discuss how a religious believer might answer an atheist's challenge that the existence of different holy books proves that God does not exist. Record your findings.

∞ links

Look back to your research on page 9 to remind yourself what is meant by the term 'blasphemous'.

See pages 86–87 to investigate the topic of censorship in more detail.

B *The Roman Catholic Church lifted the ban on Galileo's writings in 1718*

Activities

1 Explain the impact religious literature might have on a believer.

2 Explain the impact religious literature might have on a non-believer.

∞ links

See pages 84–85 to find out more about censorship in the media.

Extension activity

1 a Using the internet, find out if the religion(s) you are studying has banned any literature because it was considered blasphemous.

   b Explain why the literature was considered to be blasphemous.

Summary

You should now be able to discuss the impact of religious literature on believers and non-believers.

wrath;
do not fret—it leads only to evil.
⁹For evil men will be cut off,
but those who hope in the LORD will
inherit the land.

¹⁰A little while, and the wicked will be no
more;

he makes his steps firm;
²⁴though he stumble, he will not fall,
for the LORD upholds him with his
hand.

²⁵I was young and now I am old,
yet I have never seen the righteous
forsaken

upright;
there is a future for the man of peace.
all sinners will be destroyed;
the future of the wicked will be cut off.

The salvation of the righteous comes
from the LORD;
stronghold in time of trouble

those who would harm me talk of my
ruin;
all day long they plot deception.

¹³I am like a deaf man, who cannot hear,
like a mute, who cannot open his
mouth;
¹⁴I have become like

3.9   What does religious literature tell us about God, belief and the writer?

■ What does religious literature tell us about God?

For Buddhists, religious literature tells them that there is no God and that they must seek enlightenment and nirvana for themselves. For the other religions, the holy books are proof of God's existence by the very fact that God has sent the revelations to believers. The emphasis of the holy books is that God is beyond human understanding. Therefore, little can be known about him and he has sent the revelations to help humans learn and understand more about him.

To help believers develop some understanding of God's message, there are commentaries and other teachings related to the holy books. For example, Hindus believe in the one God, Brahman, who appears in many aspects in the world. It is mainly though the accounts of the involvement of the gods and goddesses in the world that Hindus learn more about Brahman. For Sikhs, the Guru Granth Sahib is considered the Supreme Spiritual Authority and Head of the Sikh religion and contains not only the writings of its own religious founders, but also writings of people from other religions. As the living Guru of the Sikhs, the book is held in great reverence by Sikhs and treated with the utmost respect because it provides them with guidance and support throughout their lives.

■ What does religious literature tell us about belief?

Religious literature explains the teachings of a specific religion and this can help the members of that faith to understand more about their beliefs. It can also help those who are not believers to learn more about the beliefs of the religion.

Accounts of events within the religion can be a source of support that gives people the strength of belief to cope with hardship, suffering and persecution. In extreme circumstances, this strength can lead to a willingness to die for their beliefs. It can also show that accepting religious beliefs is more than attending a place of worship and involves accepting a total way of life, including care and concern for others. For example, when a Muslim reads about the lives of the early followers of Muhammad, they are provided with examples of how the message of the Qur'an and the teachings of the prophet are to be put into practice. The same is true in the other religions we have studied.

Religious literature may often show that there is disagreement not only between religions, but within religions about the way the beliefs of the faith are to be understood. For example, there are two main divisions in Buddhism, one called Mahayana and the other called Theravada. Each division has developed different understandings of the way to achieve enlightenment, and have different writings to support these beliefs.

Objectives

Investigate what religious literature tells us about God, belief and the writer.

Discussion activity

1   'Religious literature is only of value to those who are members of the religion to which it belongs' Do you agree? Give reasons for your answer, showing that you have thought about more than one point of view.

∞ links

See pages 24–25 and pages 46–47 to read about what art and architecture tells us about God and belief.

Extension activity

Using the internet and/or a library, find out more about the ways in which the religious literature in the religion(s) you are studying should be used and interpreted.

What does religious literature tell us about the writer?

Where the writer is recording personal revelations and spiritual experiences, there is usually a clear indication of the writer's religious beliefs. This is particularly true when the writing is a commentary or discussion of aspects of the religion to which he or she belongs.

In works of fiction, drama or poetry, it may be possible to understand the message that the writer is seeking to convey, but it may not be so easy to recognise their religious beliefs or even whether they have any beliefs at all without knowing something about their background. However, it may be possible to understand the writer's message about topics such as good and evil, living in harmony with others or helping people less fortunate than ourselves.

A *It has been suggested that the* Harry Potter *books are religious literature*

Activity

1 Choose a piece of religious literature in a religion you have studied.

a Explain what it tells you about God.

b Explain what it tells you about belief.

c Explain what it tells you about the writer.

Summary

You should now be able to explain what religious literature tells us about God, belief and the writer.

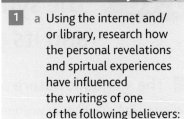

Research activity

1 a Using the internet and/or library, research how the personal revelations and spirtual experiences have influenced the writings of one of the following believers:

■ Ajahn Brahmavamoso's *The Worm* (Buddhism)

■ John Bunyan's *Pilgrims Progess* (Christianity)

■ Poetry of Swami Vivekanandra (Hinduism)

■ Poetry of Jalalud'din Rumi (Islam)

■ Allen Ginsberg's 'Kadish' (Judaism)

■ Poetry of Guru Nanak (Sikhism)

b Write an account of the message that the writer has tried to convey in their work of literature.

Discussion activity

2 As a whole class, discuss whether or not you think that the Harry Potter books tell us anything about J.K. Rowling's religious beliefs. Record your findings.

AQA *Examiner's tip*

Make sure that you understand the differences between what religious literature can tell us about God, belief and the writer.

wrath;
do not fret—it leads only to evil.
⁹For evil men will be cut off,
but those who hope in the LORD will
inherit the land.

¹⁰A little while, and the wicked will be no
more;

he makes his steps firm;
²⁴though he stumble, he will not fall,
for the LORD upholds him with his
hand.

²⁵I was young and now I am old,
yet I have never seen the righteous
forsaken

Consider the blameless, observe the
upright;
there is a future for the man of peace.
²⁸but all sinners will be destroyed;
the future of the wicked will be cut off.

The salvation of the righteous comes
from the LORD;
⁴⁰he is their stronghold in time of trouble

who seek my life set their traps,
those who would harm me talk of my
ruin;
all day long they plot deception.

¹³I am like a deaf man, who cannot hear,
like a mute, who cannot open his
mouth;
¹⁴I have become like

3.10 The symbolic nature of religious literature and its place in the modern world

■ The symbolic nature of religious literature

Religious literature has to use human language, which is inadequate for dealing with the spiritual issues involved. In addition, these issues, often claiming to be beyond human understanding, raise questions that have no certain answers. Symbolism, therefore, helps to point people towards the meaning that the writer is trying to communicate. It is often used in stories (myths) to help people understand or answer philosophical and religious questions. The story of the creation of the world is a good example.

Case study

A creation story from Hinduism

Before the world was created, there was no time and no space, just an endless ocean. In the nothingness, a giant cobra floated on the surface and within its endless coils the god Vishnu lay asleep. Everything was peaceful and silent. Suddenly a humming sound – Om – began to fill the emptiness and silence. The water began to shake and Vishnu woke up. Light began to enter the darkness. A lotus flower began to grow out of Vishnu and in the centre of the blossom sat Brahman. Vishnu told Brahman that it was time to create the world and the process of creation began. Brahman divided the lotus flower into three: one part became the heavens; one part the sky; and one part the earth. On the earth, he created vegetation, followed by life in the sea, on the land and in the sky. Finally, he made humans.

A *Can non-Hindus understand the symbolism of Hindu creation stories?*

Objectives

Investigate the symbolic nature of religious literature.

Investigate the place of religious literature in the modern world.

∞ links

Look back to page 26 to remind yourself of what is meant by symbolic nature.

Discussion activity

With a partner, in a small group or as a whole class, discuss the symbolism of the creation story from Hinduism. Record your findings.

∞ links

Look back to page 12 to remind yourself of the meaning of symbolism.

Sometimes familiar objects are used to help understanding. In Sikhism, the literature teaches that God created the whole universe, and all that existed before creation was God. While alone, God planned the universe and then when God had finished the planning, everything needed for creation was enclosed in an egg. When God decided that the time was right, the shell burst and the elements to create the universe started to move out and away from the point of bursting.

Understanding the symbols of religious literature

The understanding of religious literature depends upon personal interpretation of particular words and symbols. The extent of a person's knowledge and understanding of the religion will also influence their reading of the religious literature. For example, a person who does not have any knowledge of Christian teaching will fail to see the connection between the death and coming back to life of the lion Aslan in *The Lion, the Witch and the Wardrobe* and the death and resurrection of Jesus. However, they will probably understand the battle between good and evil, which could be the beginnings of becoming more receptive to spiritual ideas.

The place of religious literature in the modern world

Holy books and other works, intended to help believers understand their faith, have a place in the modern world for the religion to which they belong. Within the religions we have studied, the literature still helps believers to understand their faith and strengthen their beliefs. The holy books are still central to the worship, as are writings explaining them. For example, the Bible is still one of the bestselling books in the world.

B   *The Bible is still a bestselling book*

However, for people who are not attending places of worship, religious literature has less influence and little relevance to everyday life. Reading is less popular, especially with young people, and so there is less chance that religious literature will inspire people to accept religious ideas.

Many religious writers still believe that it is through literature, especially drama, that religious ideas can be expressed, so that people will think about those beliefs and may even join a group of believers or change their lifestyle.

AQA   *Examiner's tip*

Make sure that you understand what is meant by symbolism.

Activities

1   Explain the importance of symbolism to religious literature, supporting your answer with examples.

2   'You can only understand the symbols in religious literature if you are a member of that faith tradition.' Do you agree? Give reasons for your answer, showing that you have thought about more than one point of view.

Summary

You should now be able to discuss both the symbolic nature of religious literature and its place in the modern world.

3

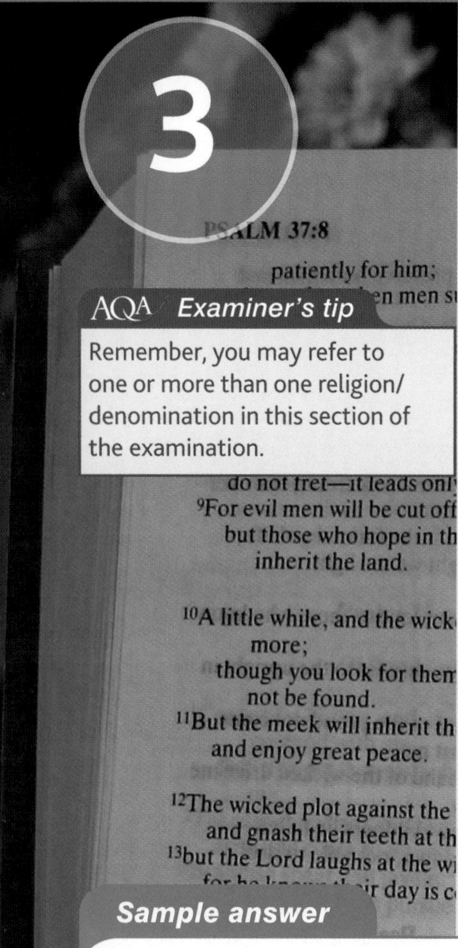

PSALM 37:8

patiently for him;
...en men s...

do not fret—it leads onl...
⁹For evil men will be cut off
    but those who hope in th
        inherit the land.

¹⁰A little while, and the wick
        more;
    though you look for them
        not be found.
¹¹But the meek will inherit th
    and enjoy great peace.

¹²The wicked plot against the
    and gnash their teeth at th
¹³but the Lord laughs at the w
    for he know... ...ir day is c...

Religion and literature – summary

For the examination you should now be able to:

✔ explain what is meant by 'spirituality' and 'religious literature'

✔ explain how religious literature is produced – through inspiration, revelation or devotion

✔ describe and explain different types of religious literature, including holy books, books of teachings of famous believers, fiction with a religious message and poetry

✔ describe and explain how and why religions use literature

✔ explain how religious literature is used in public and private worship

✔ explain the impact of religious literature on believers and non-believers

✔ explain what religious literature tells us about God, belief and the writer

✔ explain the symbolic nature of religious literature

✔ evaluate the place of religious literature in the modern world.

Sample answer

1   Write an answer to the following examination question:

'God is revealed most clearly through religious art.' Do you agree? Give reasons for your answer, showing that you have thought about more than one point of view. Refer to religious arguments in your answer.

(6 marks)

2   Read the following sample answer:

> As no one reads books anymore, then religious literature is outdated. Also, no one goes to places of worship so they don't read their holy books. Books written about religion are old fashioned and difficult to understand and they do not agree with each other, so they only prove

> to people that God does not exist. The same goes for plays. As no one goes to the theatre, then drama is another form of religious literature that is outdated in the modern world. People are more interested in playing computer games than reading religious literature. No one is interested.

3   With a partner, discuss the sample answer. Do you think that there are other things that the student could have included in the answer?

4   What mark would you give this answer out of 6? (Look at the mark scheme in the Introduction on page 7 (AO2) before you attempt this.) What are the reasons for the mark you have given?

AQA Examination-style questions

1 Look at the photograph and answer the following questions.

(a) Name **two** examples of religious literature. (*2 marks*)

Make sure that you name **two** examples. If you only give one, you will only get a maximum of 1 mark.

(b) Briefly explain three different kinds of religious literature. (*3 marks*)

Explain **three** different kinds of religious literature to gain a maximum of 1 mark for each.

(c) 'Religious literature has a very powerful influence on people.'
What do you think? Explain your opinion. (*3 marks*)

Remember that even if you are asked for your opinion, you will actually get marks for the **reasons** you give. You are not being asked to give an alternative point of view.

(d) Religious literature is said to be inspired or revealed.
Explain what is meant by 'inspired' **and** 'revealed'. (*4 marks*)

Make sure that you explain each word in relation to religious literature.

(e) 'God is revealed most clearly through religious books.' Do you agree?
Give reasons for your answer, showing that you have thought about
more than one point of view. Refer to religious arguments in your answer. (*6 marks*)

Make sure that you include examples to support your points. For example, when you explain different kinds of religious literature, such as holy books or accounts of the lives of holy people, provide examples such as the Qur'an or the Pali Canon.

4 Religion and the media

4.1 What is the media?

Defining the media

The **media** have a great influence on our society. They include newspapers, magazines, analogue, satellite and digital television, the internet, films and documentaries – all things we take for granted in modern Britain.

Objectives

Understand the meaning of the term 'the media'.

Evaluate the power of different sources of media.

AQA *Examiner's tip*

Make sure that you state which type of media you are referring to.

Key terms

Media: the means of conveying information to the public, especially television, newspapers and the internet.

A Some different forms of media

What do the media do?

The media perform many functions. These include:

- education – we use media to learn
- information – the media inform us about such things as current affairs
- entertainment – people expect the media to entertain them
- influence and persuasion – many forms of media try to influence our way of thinking or try to persuade us that one idea or product is better than another.

Activity

1 a   With a partner, write these **four** functions of the media in order of importance:

   - education
   - information
   - entertainment
   - influence and persuasion.

   b   Explain the reasons for your chosen order.

   c   Can you think of any other functions the media perform?

■ The power of the media

Malcolm X (1925–1965), the Islamic American Civil Rights leader, once said:

> **66** *The media's the most powerful entity on earth. They have the power to make the innocent guilty and to make the guilty innocent… because they control the minds of the masses.* **99**
>
> *Malcolm X*

B   *Malcolm X*

The media Malcolm X was speaking about was very different from the media we know now. At the time of his death, there were very few television channels and most programmes were still in black and white. Personal computers and the internet had not been invented. Malcolm X was referring mainly to newspapers, magazines and radio. However, if his statement was correct in the middle of the 20th century, it might still be correct at the beginning of the 21st century.

Many people are concerned about the way the media influence people's lives. For example, a person who reads a newspaper that is biased towards a particular political party may be influenced to vote for that party. If this is true, the owner of a newspaper is able to wield great power. In 1997, Rupert Murdoch's 'News International' media group, which includes *The Sun* newspaper, made a decision to support the British Labour party in the general election of that year. This ensured that Labour's campaign to win the election was reported favourably and readers of *The Sun* were encouraged to vote Labour. Labour did in fact win the election and Tony Blair became Prime Minister, replacing the Conservative John Major. Of course, Rupert Murdoch may have had no influence at all, but many political commentators believe that he did and that, equally, he had previously influenced the election of the Conservative party.

If the media can exercise power in this way, there would appear to be nothing that newspapers, television and the internet cannot influence, including religion.

Activity

2   Is the statement by Malcolm X true in the 21st century? Give reasons for your answer, along with examples.

Activities

3   'The media can greatly influence people.' Do you agree? Give reasons for your answer, showing that you have thought about more than one point of view.

4   Is there anything that the media cannot influence?

5   Which part of the media (newspaper, magazine, TV, internet, films, documentary) do you think is the most powerful? Explain your answer.

Summary

You should now be able to identify different forms of media and their purposes, and also evaluate their power.

C   *Tony Blair, British Prime Minister 1997–2007*

4.2 How is religion portrayed on television?

The law governing religion on television

"Not more hymn-singing on the TV!"

"Yes, I'm sure there was some on last Sunday as well."

A

Religious programming is governed by law, and Ofcom (the Office of Communications) is responsible for ensuring that the regulations are not broken. Ofcom has the power to fine television channels or close them down completely if a complaint is sufficiently serious or previous warnings have not been heeded.

The amount of time religious programmes take up on **terrestrial television** (analogue and digital) is strictly controlled. Programmes that try to promote a faith or recruit followers are not allowed. No programme can allow members of one faith group to denigrate or put down another. Religious programming on terrestrial television tends to be connected with Christian worship, often on the main channels (e.g. *Songs of Praise*), or documentaries on religious topics, mainly on Channels 4 and 5.

Secular programmes **are** allowed to make denigrating comments about religious faith, despite the fact that such comments may cause offence. However, content that may cause the most offence is usually edited out.

Satellite broadcasting channels do not have to follow these rules because they are not regulated by British law. Therefore, there are several channels devoted to programmes that support believers and try to recruit more (e.g. God Channel, Inspiration and Islam Channel).

■ The portrayal of religion on television

Many people find religious broadcasting helpful, informative and interesting. *Songs of Praise* on BBC1, as well as 'Thought for the Day' on the *Today* programme and the 'Daily Service', both on BBC Radio 4, are popular with parts of the population. Worship-based programmes can be helpful to people who cannot physically attend places of worship, and Muslims welcome the televising of prayers and readings from the Qur'an. Documentaries on a wide range of faiths help to educate people and may promote more tolerance and understanding to combat prejudice.

However, the portrayal of religion is not always positive. Some programmes deliberately mock God or religious leaders. Many people thought that *Jerry Springer – The Opera*, shown by the BBC on 8 January 2005, was an example of that. There was huge opposition from Christians complaining about the obscenities it contained and, more importantly to them, the perceived mocking of Jesus and God, which some interpreted as blasphemy.

The inaccurate portrayal of Muslims as terrorists on a variety of secular programmes from news through to documentaries and comedy has also caused widespread offence. Some people believe that news reporting is biased in favour of some religions and against others, and could possibly contribute to prejudice and even violence and terrorism. If a person is told something that is wrong enough times, they may end up believing it and act upon this belief, despite it being wrong.

In soap operas and comedies, Christian characters are often figures of fun or portrayed as being extreme, rather than in a positive and sympathetic light. In crime dramas, serial killers may even be presented as having religious motivations for their awful actions. In the BBC soap opera *EastEnders*, Dot Cotton is rarely taken seriously because of her Christian faith and her regularly quoting the Bible. However, her religious beliefs were very relevant in one of the most sensitive episodes when she agonised over the ethical question of euthanasia in relation to her best friend Ethel.

Christian priests are often portrayed as stereotypes. Although in the Channel 4 comedy *Father Ted*, the priests sometimes come across as being irreligious; elsewhere, priests are often portrayed as being old and a bit eccentric. In *The Simpsons*, Ned Flanders, who has a religious faith, is characterised as being even more odd than the other characters.

∞ links

See pages 86–87 to find out how religion is portrayed in film and on the internet.

B   *Jerry Springer – The Opera*

∞ links

The topic of blasphemy is dealt with in more detail on pages 84–85. See the Glossary at the back of the book for a definition.

> **Extension activity**
>
> In your opinion, what sorts of offences should Ofcom punish broadcasters for?

> **AQA   Examiner's tip**
>
> Make sure that you name the programme title when referring to characters and storylines.

Activities

3   List some religious characters on television who are portrayed in a positive and sympathetic way.

4   Note down some of the positive aspects of television coverage of religion.

5   'Religion should always be portrayed positively on television.' Do you agree? Give reasons for your answer, showing that you have thought about more than one point of view.

> **Summary**
>
> You should now be able to explain how coverage of religion on television is regulated, and discuss how religion and religious people are portrayed on television.

A   *Dawn French as Geraldine Grainger, the fictional Vicar of Dibley*

Objectives

Study a television comedy focused on religion.

Evaluate the effect the programme has on real life.

Activity

1   Explain why it was a brave decision to start this comedy series about a female priest in 1994.

Case study

Background

The Vicar of Dibley was written by Richard Curtis and Paul Mayhew Archer (both well-known comedy writers) and starred Dawn French in the title role. It was broadcast on BBC1 in 20 episodes, split into three series, starting in 1994, with Christmas specials in 1996, 1997, 2004 and 2006 and the final episode on New Year's Day 2007. It has been regularly repeated on BBC1 and satellite channels since.

The storyline

The Vicar of Dibley is set in a small village in rural Oxfordshire. The first episode deals with the appointment of a new vicar and the reaction of the eccentric residents of Dibley. Taking advantage of a historic ruling by the Church of England in 1992 that allowed women to become priests for the first time, the writers decided that the replacement vicar for Dibley should not be the stereotypical comedy vicar, but a larger than life woman called Geraldine Grainger. As

the series developed, Geraldine was shown to have a passion for chocolate and to be on the lookout for a good-looking husband (stereotypical of women, but not of vicars). While there is no doubting the sincerity of her faith, she has a great sense of humour, which she is not afraid to use in her discussion of religion. This outlook and her interactions with the scatterbrained verger Alice provide some of the best comedy moments in the show. Some of the humour is a bit irreverent, but it is gentle and never becomes offensive.

After the idea of a female vicar caused initial horror amongst the villagers, Geraldine won them around and became integrated into the small insular community. The storylines in the early episodes where she struggles to be accepted establish some strong characters from the supporting cast, some of whom are complete stereotypes of rural life. In the final programme, Geraldine marries a handsome newcomer to Dibley, after having turned down marriage proposals from most of the men in the village.

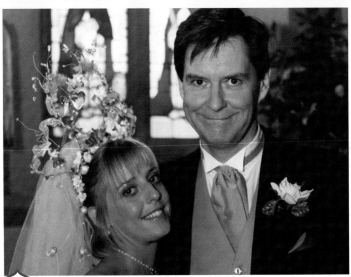

B   *Alice and Hugo marry in Dibley Parish Church*

◼ The impact of the programme

It might have been a brave decision to broadcast a comedy programme about a female priest just two years after the Church of England allowed women to become priests. At that time, there was still a lot of opposition to the decision from within the Church. However, there was little opposition to the programme from either Christians or non-Christians. In fact, the series was extremely popular. In 2004, it was voted as Britain's third best situation comedy (sitcom) of all time and the broadcast repeats are still watched by millions.

In 2006, for the first time, there were more women than men ordained into the Church of England priesthood (244 women and 234 men were ordained in that year). This took the overall figure of full-time salaried female clergy ordained since 1994 to 1507, excluding chaplains in such places as hospitals and universities. Obviously, there are many reasons for this increase in the ordination of women, but it is possible that *The Vicar of Dibley* helped some people to accept women priests and even encouraged some women to become ordained.

Research activity 🔍

Try to watch at least **one** episode of The Vicar of Dibley, which is widely available on DVD. The first episode considers the issue of women priests and opposition to them. Think about the reasons given for and against women priests.

Activities

2   With a partner, discuss what attitudes towards women priests you have come across.

3   How much effect do you think *The Vicar of Dibley* has had on changing people's attitudes about women priests? Give reasons for your answer.

Summary

You should now be able to discuss a popular television programme that portrays Christianity in a sensitive way, and evaluate the impact it has had on Christianity.

Different types of newspaper

In Britain, there are different styles of newspaper. *The Times*, the *Daily Telegraph*, the *Guardian* and *The Independent* are called broadsheet newspapers. They see their role as informing the public with their news, sport and lifestyle stories and expressing opinion on current affairs in longer articles. Although they may be biased towards a certain political opinion, these newspapers usually try to report events accurately.

Occupying the middle ground are the *Daily Mail* and the *Daily Express*, which also report serious news, together with stories of general human interest. They also have a focus on lifestyle issues.

The Sun, the *Daily Mirror,* the *Daily Sport* and the *Daily Star* are called red-top tabloids (after the red background to their names) and are at the opposite end of the spectrum from the broadsheets. They focus mainly on celebrity culture, with brief coverage of news events. They use snappy headlines and print controversial gossip-style stories, and, in the case of *The Sun*, a topless page 3 model. In terms of daily sales, red-top tabloids are much more popular than the other papers.

Newspaper portrayal of moral issues

This headline in source **A** appeared on the front page of *The Sun* on 4 May 1982. It was reporting a British attack on an Argentine gunboat the ARA Alferez Sobral, which was badly damaged with the loss of eight lives. Shortly before that, a British nuclear submarine, *HMS Conquerer*, had fired missiles that sunk the military cruiser *ARA General Belgrano* with the loss of 323 lives. Around 700 others were rescued from the sea after the sinking.

These two events were confused by *The Sun*, which reported that the cruiser had sunk and the *General Belgrano* had been damaged. As they believed that the loss of life was much lower, they ran the headline in their first edition. Once their error became clear, the headline was changed in later editions to 'Did 1200 Argies drown?'

A *The Sun, 4 May 1982*

Activities

4   Do people copy the bad behaviour of celebrities? Explain your opinion.

5   'The more times unacceptable behaviour is reported, the more acceptable it becomes.' Do you agree? Give reasons for your answer, showing that you have thought about more than one point of view.

Another issue that people may have with the tabloid newspapers and mazagines of a similar style, such as *OK!* and *Hello!*, is their reporting on celebrities' lifestyles. They tend to focus on reporting bad behaviour, which raises questions about whether they are invading the celebrities' privacy and whether they are glamourising such behaviour, which ordinary people may copy.

Portrayal of religion

British newspapers and magazines are usually quite careful not to cause offence over religious content. The editors realise that if they print stories critical of a particular religion, they may cause offence and could even be breaking the law. Magazines such as *Private Eye* make fun of politics, personalities and religion, but not in a cruel way that people may object to. However, as good news doesn't sell copies, stories in newspapers and magazines, including religious ones, tend to focus on when things go wrong. For example, a story about a priest behaving inappropriately is more likely to be reported than a good news story about religion.

B   *A selection of headlines*

Activity

6   Why do you think newspapers are quite careful not to offend religious believers? Give reasons for your answer.

Extension activity

Using the internet and/or a library, find some newspaper stories that have religious themes or content. How do they portray religion?

All religions in Britain produce their own newspapers or journals, either in print or online. *The Jewish Chronicle*, *The Muslim News* and the Christian *Church Times* and *The Tablet* are examples of printed newspapers.

Research activity

Using the internet, search for newspapers and journals from the religion(s) you are studying. Study the types of story published and the way in which they are reported.

Summary

You should now be able to discuss how religious and moral issues are portrayed in different types of newspapers or magazines.

The power to cause offence

The publication of religiously sensitive material can cause offence to religious people. This was shown very dramatically in 2005–6 when 12 cartoons of the prophet Muhammad were published and controversy followed.

Case study

The Muhammad cartoons

On 30 September 2005, a Danish newspaper published 12 cartoons of the prophet Muhammad. Some were quite gentle in their message, but others seemed deliberately provocative. One of them even portrayed him as a terrorist. They were published to highlight self-censorship after a Danish writer complained that he could not find an illustrator for a children's book about Muhammad. The reason was that Islam forbids images of Allah, Muhammad or any of the other prophets.

Two weeks after publication of the cartoons, nearly 3,500 people demonstrated peacefully against the newspaper in Copenhagen. In addition, Islamic governments protested to the Danish government, several countries withdrew their ambassadors to Demark and Danish products were boycotted.

Nevertheless, newspapers in other European countries, starting with Austria and followed by France, Germany, Italy and Spain (but not Britain) went on to republish the cartoons. Protests grew, some of which became violent. In Syria and Lebanon, embassies and consulates belonging to Denmark, Sweden and Chile were stormed and set on fire. As the violence grew, over 100 people died, many killed when the police in several cities opened fire on violent demonstrators.

Denmark's prime minister referred to the controversy as 'Denmark's worst international crisis since the Second World War' and, on 2 February 2006, went on Arabic television to apologise for the offence caused by the publication of the cartoons. However, he also defended the right to freedom of expression.

Eventually the protests died down, partly through more moderate Muslims urging Muslims who took offence not to react in a violent and non-Islamic way. They were persuaded to accept that the Muhammad cartoons, while unfortunate, were similar to cartoons produced in the Arab and Islamic press aimed at Israel and America, often using Jewish and Christian imagery. A weekly newspaper in Jordan (an Islamic country) even went so far as to publish some of the cartoons itself.

A *The Danish flag is burned in a demonstration*

Activity

1   a   With a partner, discuss whether you think it is right for a non-Muslim to draw images of Muhammad, which Muslims are forbidden to do. Write down your reasons.

    b   Do you think that newspapers in other countries were justified in publishing pictures that had previously caused offence? Explain your opinion.

    c   Why do you think that no British newspaper published the cartoons?

Discussion activity 👥👥👥

1   With a partner, in a small group or as a whole class, discuss the following statement: 'Newspapers should be allowed "freedom of expression".' Do you agree? Give reasons for your answer, showing that you have thought about more than one point of view.

AQA   *Examiner's tip*

If you get the opportunity to refer to the prophet Muhammad cartoons as an example of the way religion is portrayed in the press, do not forget to mention the fact that the majority of papers and magazines did not print them.

■ The power to influence

All forms of the media have great power to influence the actions and decisions of ordinary people. Questions about how the media use this power are particularly important when their audience is impressionable young people. Glossy 'teen' magazines make an interesting example, especially as there is no lower age restriction on who can buy them.

Many 'teen' magazines portray a glamorous way of life that most readers can only dream of. Images of size zero models wearing expensive clothes have been blamed for young girls developing eating disorders in trying to achieve the same look, even though it would be physiologically impossible for many of them. So, even though their main aim is to provide their readers with enjoyment and education, repeated emphasis on a certain type of lifestyle could be seen as a type of **indoctrination** – encouraging young people into a particular way of thinking.

Key terms

Indoctrination: to repeatedly stress ideas or beliefs in the hope that they will be accepted without thinking.

Some magazines for both males (e.g. *Nuts* and *Zoo*) and females (e.g. *Bliss* and *Sugar*) contain problem pages, which focus on relationship issues, and articles that are sexually explicit. Religious people might object to these features because they do not reflect religious teachings about chastity (no sex) before marriage and can be read by young people under 16, the legal age of sexual consent. Articles about contraception are against the teachings of Roman Catholics and Orthodox Jews among others.

B   *A selection of teen magazines*

Activity

2   a   Explain why some religious people are concerned about young people reading 'teen' magazines.

   b   Do you think they are right to be concerned? Give reasons for your answer.

Discussion activity 👥👥👥

2   With a partner, in a small group or as a whole class, discuss the following statement: 'It is no surprise that young people reading teen magazines believe that sex before marriage or with assorted partners is the norm and feel left out if they are not part of it.' Do you agree? Give reasons for your answer, showing that you have thought about more than one point of view.

Summary

You should now be able to discuss the power of the press in relation to religious and moral issues. You should also be able to refer to a specific example to support your points.

What is censorship?

Discussion activity

Imagine that you have found out that there is going to be a feature on television about you. It is going to say nasty things about you that are **not** true.

With a partner, discuss how you would feel about this. What would you do about it? Record your findings.

Censorship takes place when a broadcaster or publisher is pressurised, usually by an official group or independent individual, to cut out parts of a film, programme, article, report or book that the group or individual feels should not be seen or read. The reasons can vary. For example in Britain, films and television programmes are often censored to protect younger viewers from seeing or hearing unsuitable material. Censorship can also be for political reasons. Most democracies use it in the interests of national security, especially in times of war. However, other kinds of governments such as dictatorships may censor the news, for example, to prevent the public from knowing what is going on politically so they cannot take action against the situation.

Blasphemy

Another justification for censorship is blasphemy – a type of censorship on religious grounds. The blasphemy laws covering Christianity were abolished in England and Wales on 8 July 2008. However, on 29 June 2007, the European parliament introduced a law prohibiting blasphemy, insults and hate speech against persons on grounds of their faith in any religion. This European law now applies in Britain.

In 2007, a group called Christian Voice attempted to prosecute the BBC over its broadcasting of *Jerry Springer – The Opera* on the grounds of blasphemy. The group's attempts were thrown out by the courts because the blasphemy laws did not extend to stage productions or broadcasts of them. Thus, they did not get the chance to have a ruling on whether the BBC's broadcast was blasphemous or not.

Blasphemy raises serious issues about potential conflicts between religious teachings and national and international law. Every religion that believes in a god, teaches that believers must not to talk or behave in a way that insults God. Hindus pay God immense respect in worship (puja) by making offerings and removing their shoes in God's presence. Sikhs also remove their shoes while in the gurdwara and are respectful to the Guru Granth Sahib (God's final guru) by, for example, approaching it, bowing towards it and not turning their backs on it. Christians, Jews and Muslims obey the commandment not to 'misuse the name of the Lord your God' (Exodus 20:7).

Objectives

Understand the purpose of censorship, especially on television.

Understand the term 'blasphemy'.

Evaluate the need for censorship to protect religious believers.

A Indecent images are censored

Key terms

Censorship: when a group (often the state) do not let the public have access to certain things, often relating to the media.

⃝⃝ links

Look back to pages 82–83 for an example that some interpreted to be blasphemy.

⃝⃝ links

Look back to page 77 for more about *Jerry Springer – The Opera*.

■ Censorship of television

Because television is transmitted into virtually every home in Britain and, with digital or satellite TV, hundreds of stations can be available at the press of a button, many people are concerned that they have insufficient control over what appears on their television. This is especially so if they have young children because they will probably want to control what their children see (which could be seen as a form of censorship).

The 'nine o'clock watershed' is designed to prevent bad language, sexual content or violence being broadcast before 9pm when children may be watching. It is an effective form of control that most people are in favour of. After the watershed, some nudity, bad language and a degree of violence can be shown, but there are still strict controls. For example, although it is not illegal to show sexual scenes, images that show penetration during intercourse are not legal. This also applies to specialist pay-to-view sex channels on satellite and digital. Films have to be edited to comply with the law governing television broadcasts, even though they may be acceptable with an 18 certificate in the cinema.

News and documentary programmes may be censored in the interests of national security or if there is a fear of misrepresentation or libel (broadcasting a false statement that damages a person's reputation). Reporting of legal processes is also strictly controlled, including a ban on naming offenders under the age of 16.

B

Summary

You should now be able to evaluate the need for censorship and whether religion should have the right to censor the media.

Censorship and religious influence

◼ Film censorship

There is strict censorship on films, which works through **categorisation of films**. This is designed to ensure that children and young people do not watch films that are deemed unsuitable for them because of sex, violence, drug taking or bad language. Film producers may have to cut some scenes out of a film if they want it classified as suitable for a certain age group.

Enforcement of this classification system is left up to individual cinemas. They will not knowingly allow children to watch a film that is classified as unsuitable for them. When the film is released on DVD, the same age restrictions apply to its rental and sale. However, once the DVD is in the home, it is up to parents to say whether or not their children may watch a film.

Indicating films are suitable for:

 (1) All

 (2) All, but recommended for children over the age of 4

 (3) All, but recommended for children over the age of 8

 (4) Young people over 12 years, but under 12s can view it if accompanied by a parent

 (5) Over 12s only

 (6) Over 15s only

 (7) Over 18s only

R18 *(8) Over 18s, licensed cinemas and sex shops only*

B *Film classifications*

A *Stickers advising of bad language appear on CDs*

Key terms

Categorisation of films: the way in which films are given certificates to ensure that only people for whom the film is suitable get to see it.

Activity

1. a Explain the system of film classification.
   b Does film classification work effectively? Explain your opinion.

Research activity

Find out more about film classification at www.bbfc.co.uk

◼ Religious influences on films

All religions teach peace, modesty and faithfulness (forbidding adultery). Therefore, films that show violence and sex are rejected by most believers. These values can be embraced by some film makers, like those working on Bollywood films in Mumbai. Bollywood films are generally romantic musicals set in Hindu society in India. They reflect the Hindu way of life and therefore are usually suitable for family viewing because they do not contain bad language, violence or nudity. Their popularity is growing throughout the world, not just with Hindu audiences.

AQA Examiner's tip

Use the religious principles of peace, modesty and faithfulness if you are giving a religious argument against films showing explicit sex or extreme violence.

Film makers are generally quite careful not to misrepresent religion, although they often include language that is offensive, usually to Christianity, but sometimes to religious believers in general. However, many Christians protested when the film *The Life of Brian* came out in 1979. Given a 15 certificate, it paralleled the life of Jesus (although the makers denied any links with Jesus). Opinion between Christians was divided, but it has more recently been shown several times on television with little objection.

▋ Internet censorship

Despite the massive benefits people derive from the internet, it also has its sinister side. Sir Tim Berners-Lee, who built the world's first website, recognised this in 2008 when he announced the setting up of the World Wide Web Foundation, aimed at controlling 'malicious rumours and conspiracy theories' on the internet.

However, the internet is very difficult to control. Anyone can post anything on it, even if the material breaks laws, has immoral purposes or offends religious beliefs. However, the person who breaks the law will have to face the legal consequences when caught.

It is easier to control what material can be downloaded from the internet. For example, it is an offence to download indecent images (especially those associated with paedophilia) and material that could be used in terrorism and serious crime. Parents can also use special software to restrict the types of websites their children can access.

Access to certain websites can persuade people to do things they might never have considered otherwise. On 19 September 2008, Hammaad Munshi was sentenced to two years in a young offender's institution for being in possession of material 'likely to be used for terrorist purposes'. In addition to downloading that type of material, he used messenger services to communicate with others in the group to which he had become attached. In sentencing Munshi, Judge Timothy Pontius said that he had 'brought very great shame upon yourself, your family and your religion'. Others may have the view that he was the victim of indoctrination.

A spokesperson for Munshi's family said: 'This case demonstrates how a young impressionable teenager can be groomed so easily through the internet to associate with those whose views run contrary to true Muslim beliefs and values.'

Activity

3 'It is impossible to censor the internet, so we shouldn't try'. Do you agree? Give reasons for your answer, showing that you have thought about more than one point of view.

Summary

You should now be able to discuss and evaluate censorship of films and the internet.

Activity

2 a Should film makers be allowed to misrepresent religions in films? Explain your opinion.

 b Why do you think that films whose content was considered unsuitable when released (e.g. *The Life of Brian*) are more generally accepted now?

C   *The worldwide web*

Discussion activity

With a partner, discuss whether or not the internet should be controlled by censoring websites that are:

■ untrue

■ offensive

■ terrorist-related.

Record your findings.

AQA   *Examiner's tip*

You could consider using the internet as an example to justify censorship because it shows what can happen when there is no censorship.

4.8   How and why do religions use the media?

▣ It's never been so easy

There has never been a better time for religions to communicate their message to a mass audience. In the early days of each religion, its leaders and believers had to rely on word of mouth and handwriting. Now, it is very different. For example, with the press of a key on a computer, text or an image can be sent all over the world in a matter of seconds. If you want to talk to somebody in the next town or city, you don't have to travel. All that is needed is for both of you to have a phone.

Objectives

Investigate the ways that religions use the media and why.

Evaluate the effectiveness of religions' use of the media.

Discussion activity

In silence, try to reflect on what life was like without computers, the internet and mobile phones. Discuss and record your thoughts with a partner.

▣ Use of television

Religious leaders recognise that an appearance on television is a good way of getting a message across because of the high number of people watching. For example, they may want to give a message to educate people about an ethical issue, perhaps on a discussion programme or documentary. For religions keen to convert non-believers, such as Christianity and Islam, television also provides an ideal platform for spreading their message. Satellite television allows all religions to produce programmes, broadcast to a worldwide audience, that focus on education, worship and entertainment to reflect their religious ethos and teaching.

Some Christian channels, especially those based in the USA, have received bad publicity. Jim Bakker who ran one of the largest channels, the PTL (Praise the Lord) network, was jailed in 1988 for fraud. Whilst he was in jail, his wife divorced him for his alleged adultery. Such well-publicised scandals harm the reputation of similar channels that are entirely reputable.

Of course, because satellite or digital television provides so many channels, viewers have a wide choice over what they watch. Unless they are committed to a faith, it is unlikely that they will choose to watch a specifically religious channel. However, they may take the opportunity to think about ethical and religious opinions put forward in some programmes and want to educate themselves by finding out more.

◯◯ links

Look back to pages 76–77 to remind yourself about religion on television.

A *There are now many religious TV channels*

Activity

1   'Religious television channels should not be allowed.' Do you agree? Give reasons for your answer, showing that you have thought about more than one point of view.

■ Use of the internet

The internet is widely used by all religions to provide information and assist prayer and worship. It is also used to encourage people to support charities by informing them of the work undertaken and providing the opportunity to donate money. Many individual places of worship have their own websites to keep their communities and congregations in touch with events connected with the place of worship. For example, a mosque may post the times for prayer and for sunrise and sunset to assist the Ramadan fast on its website, Buddhists may use websites for advertising meditation classes and the times when lay Buddhists can attend the vihara (temple).

E-mail has made it much easier for leaders of places of worship to fulfil their duties. For example, they can pass information on to selected people and receive prayer requests on behalf of those who are sick or suffering much more quickly and efficiently by e-mail.

■ Use of newspapers and magazines

Some coverage of religious topics in newspapers and magazines is very positive and might be welcomed or encouraged by the religions concerned. Religious content often appears as topical features, like an article on the festival of Diwali, which gives a wide audience the chance to find out more. It also provides useful understanding as background information to reports about ethical or religious issues.

Specific religious newspapers and magazines such as the *Church Times*, *The Tablet* and *The Muslim News*, are published to educate followers about issues that relate to their faith, and provide information specific to the faith such as explaining passages from holy books. However, they will have limited appeal to non-believers.

B   *Websites broadcast continuous live feeds from the Western Wall in Jerusalem*

∞ links

Look back to pages 80–81 for more information about newspapers and magazines.

AQA   *Examiner's tip*

Remember, if writing about how local places of worship use the internet, you can use local examples.

Activities

2   Explain how and why religions use the media. Focus on the roles of informing people, gaining new followers and assisting worship.

3   Which type of media do you think is the most effective way for religions to get their message across? Explain your opinion.

Summary

You should now be able to discuss how religions use the media and assess the media's effectiveness.

4.9 — What do religious media tell us about God, belief and media producers?

What do religious media tell us about God?

The media give mixed messages about God. The specifically religious media, both written and broadcast, tend to portray him as a loving God who is deserving of the worship of his people. He is approachable but makes demands on them to live in a way that is moral and just. Some of the presenters on the evangelical Christian television channels see themselves as specially chosen by God to pass on his message to a wide audience. Islamic TV channels tend to be much more scholarly, discussing interpretations of the Qur'an and the challenges of being a Muslim. The five daily prayers are broadcast live for people at home to join in.

Even though there are lots of TV channels that people can choose to watch, some see the religious channels as a way of indoctrinating non-believers into believing in God. This would only be the case if people were forced to watch them. Most believers who use the media to pass on their ideas to others do so responsibly, taking the opportunity to do what they feel is their duty to God by educating themselves and others about him.

The secular media (which has no specific religious purpose) cannot be seen to promote one religious belief or another, but they also have to be careful not to promote an anti-God agenda because they would soon lose viewers, listeners or readers who were believers.

Objectives

Investigate what religious media tell us about God, belief and the people who produce articles or programmes for the media.

A Some religious TV channels use the media to preach

Discussion activity

With a partner, discuss the following statement: 'Promoting belief in God should be banned from television.' Do you agree? Give reasons for your answer, showing that you have thought about more than one point of view.

What do religious media tell us about belief?

The media at large are not as sympathetic towards belief as many religious people would like them to be. In today's scientific age, for example, the media often seem to send out the message that religious belief is not enough. An increasing number of documentaries attempt to use scientific techniques to prove or disprove events and details in religious tradition or in holy books, especially relating to the Bible and the life of Jesus. While a Jew or a Christian may believe that Moses led his people across the Red Sea or that Noah's Ark rested on top of Mount Ararat when the Flood subsided, scientists and archaeologists sometimes set out to prove that such events could not have happened as told. However, their findings rarely discover the absolute truth.

B Does it matter where the events in the story of Noah's Ark took place?

On the other hand, there are also documentaries that show the nature of belief and highlight its importance in religion. In addition, of course, many religious believers think that religious stories provide important spiritual truths and are not worried about the exact historical details.

Activities

1 Is there a place for religious belief in today's increasingly scientific world? Explain your opinion.

2 Does it matter whether or not scientists disprove some details from stories in holy books? Give your reasons and then share them with a partner.

What do religious media tell us about media producers?

Although some of the people who publish, produce or broadcast the different types of religious media will not necessarily have a faith, others will be inspired to write for, or be attracted to a job in, such media because of their beliefs. Their faith will show in what they write, publish or broadcast. For example, producers and broadcasters of programmes on specifically religious channels aim to educate believers and support them in following their beliefs. Some also try to gain followers. They are also presenting a spiritual alternative to the general media, which are mainly secular and often dismissive of religion.

Funding for broadcast and written media often dictates the content and usually comes from advertising. For example, apart from the BBC, which is funded by a compulsory licence fee, most television and radio channels rely on advertising revenue. Therefore, they try to produce programmes that appeal to a large number of people in order to attract advertisers. Religious programmes are not widely popular and do not attract so much advertising. Therefore, mainstream media focus less on religious topics and specifically religious media have to rely more on donations.

Activities

3 Should funding of television, newspapers and magazines by advertising influence their content? Explain your opinion.

4 Can you think of an alternative way of funding the media other than by advertising? Explain your ideas.

Summary

You should now be able to discuss what the media tell us about God, belief and those who produce the media.

AQA   Examiner's tip

Remember, if writing about funding of television, most channels do not receive a share of the television licensing fee.

4.10 Spirituality and the media

Spiritual benefits of the media

There is a thought in all theistic religions that God has given humankind the intelligence and opportunity to develop technology for the benefit of us all. God can be seen as an active force in the world, inspiring humankind to develop new technologies – mass media being just one of them. Most believers are happy to accept the use of new technology, which has given us different forms of media, because they recognise the benefits it can bring.

As well as entertaining, the media can help to inform and educate people about all manner of topics, including spiritual and religious ones. It can enable people to learn about and enjoy art, music, literature and architecture, for example, and, in doing so, may put them in touch with their spirituality. The media can show people what is happening around the world and help them to empathise with others. They can also help believers to practise and strengthen their religious faith. After all, the media are just a way of sharing beliefs, ideas and opportunities for understanding the world.

Spirituality is often expressed in terms of awe and wonder. The power of the media and the opportunities they provide might also be seen in the same way. The opportunity to see an event broadcast as it happens from the other side of the world and shown, with sound, on a modern high-definition colour screen would amaze anybody who could travel forward in time from 70 years ago. Even watching a feature film by inserting a small silver-coloured disk into a machine and controlling it by pressing a button would cause amazement and prompt the question 'How does it work?'

The existence of the media could be interpreted symbolically to reinforce the idea that, in God's plan, human beings are the most important species on earth, capable of having a relationship with a God who has created the earth and sustains it for people to live in.

Objectives

To explore the spiritual benefits and risks of the media.

To evaluate the links between spirituality and the media.

A *Can spiritual feeling be visualised?*

∞ links

Look back to pages 8–9 to remind yourself of what is meant by spirituality.

Activities

1. Explain any links between the media and spirituality.
2. Do you think it is right to link the media and spirituality in this way? Explain your opinion.

AQA Examiner's tip

Although expressions of spirituality through art, music, literature and architecture are all topics of their own in this unit, you can use them here if you wish.

Spiritual risks of the media

However, the way the media have evolved and advanced has brought with it the opportunity to put forward ideas that are contrary to religious belief.

The biologist Richard Dawkins is a regular contributor to television, print media and the internet to oppose the belief that God created the world and promoting his own atheism. His books (e.g. *The God Delusion*) have sold in their millions across the world and his website has millions of 'hits' every year.

Although films such as *The Da Vinci Code* provide entertainment, they could be seen as based on misinterpretation and distortion of artistic expressions of spirituality taken from the Bible. Pornography in magazines and on the internet may encourage people to behave with extreme violence or not to respect the sanctity of sex or marriage.

The internet can be a huge power for evil as well as good because people with evil intentions can contribute to it just as easily as those with good intentions. Even seemingly harmless social networking sites can be used for bullying or by paedophiles 'grooming' children or young people for sex.

Discussion activity

With a partner, discuss whether the media has become too powerful. Give reasons for your answer, showing that you have thought about more than one point of view.

B   *A drop of water causes ripples*

Activity

3   Explain how the photograph of the drop of water causing ripples could relate to the media. Think for a couple of minutes before writing your answer.

Summary

You should now be able to discuss the spiritual risks and benefits of the media, and evaluate the links between spirituality and the media.

4

Religion and media – summary

For the examination you should now be able to:

✔ understand and describe what is meant by 'the media'

✔ identify different types of media in which religion is portrayed

✔ evaluate the power of the media, especially in relation to religious and moral issues

✔ explain how coverage of religion on television is regulated

✔ analyse how religion is portrayed in different types of media and the effects of such portrayal

✔ evaluate the need for censorship and whether religions should have the right to censor the media

✔ evaluate the ways religion uses the media and their effectiveness

✔ discuss what religious media tell us about God, belief and the producers of religious media

✔ evaluate the impact of religious media on believers and non-believers

✔ give examples to support your points about religion and the media

✔ evaluate the contribution the media make to spirituality.

Sample answer

1 Write an answer to the following examination question:

Explain briefly how religions use their own television channels. *(3 marks)*

2 Read the following sample answer:

> Religions use their own television channels to tell them what to believe and to try to get other people to believe as well. I don't think other people are interested in them though, so they should be closed down because they are rubbish.

3 With a partner, discuss the sample answer. Do you think that there are other things that the student could have included in the answer?

4 What mark would you give this answer out of 3? (Look at the mark scheme in the Introduction on page 7 (AO1) before you attempt this.) What are the reasons for the mark you have given?

AQA Examination-style questions

1 Look at the photograph and answer the following questions.

(a) Give **two** types of written media. *(2 marks)*

All you need to write here are two words to give two types of written media.

(b) Explain why some religious believers oppose the content of **one** of these types of written media. *(3 marks)*

This question shows that it is wise to read all the questions before you start answering them. It would be wise to choose a type of media for part (a) that you can use easily in part (b).

(c) 'The internet is more good than bad.' What do you think? Explain your opinion. *(3 marks)*

AQA Examiner's tip
Here you are asked to give your opinion. You don't have to give an alternative point of view.

(d) Explain how religion is portrayed on terrestrial television. *(4 marks)*

AQA Examiner's tip
Remember to give details. You are not asked for examples, but they would be very helpful here.

(e) 'The media are helpful to religion.' Do you agree? Give reasons for your answer, showing that you have thought about more than one point of view. Refer to religious arguments in your answer. *(6 marks)*

AQA Examiner's tip
You need to think carefully of reasons why some people think the media are helpful to religion and reasons why other people think they are not. If you have time, finish with a conclusion, without repeating yourself. You should write between 12–15 lines.

5 Religion and music

5.1 Why do people listen to music?

Music in ancient times

Carved images of musical instruments appear in ancient tombs and temples in Egypt, the earliest dating from around 1500 BCE. This is one example that shows that music was important to people in ancient times, and there is also evidence that they used music in religious practices.

In the 8th century BCE, the prophet Amos informed the people of Israel that God was not pleased with the way they lived and worshipped, and he predicted death and destruction upon them. He is reported as having said:

This tells us that 2,750 years ago people were composing songs and music. The rest of the chapter in Amos implies that they were using them in worship. However, according to Amos, in the eyes of God, living in a just and moral way was preferable to making music.

There are many earlier references to religious music and songs. For example, the Book of Psalms is often referred to as the hymn book of the Bible, having been written over a long period of time. Some psalms are believed to have been written by King David, an accomplished musician, around 1000 BCE. The Hindu Vedas, from around the same time, also contain songs. This shows that the use of songs and music in religion was not restricted to the Middle East, but also featured in India.

Objectives

Understand and evaluate the reasons why people listen to music.

Discussion activity

1   a   With a partner, discuss why you think people over 3000 years ago believed that music was important.

    b   In what ways do you think they might have used music?

Activity

1   a   Make a list of as many reasons as possible why people use music.

    b   Compare your list with a partner.

A   *Michelangelo's statue of David, before he was king*

What is the purpose of music today?

Music today has many different purposes depending, in some ways, on what type of music is being listened to. It is unlikely that a Mozart concerto would be heard at a rave and gangster rap is unlikely to be featured in the Royal Opera House.

It is likely that your list includes reasons that can be grouped as listed below. Music may:

- assist with an *activity*, e.g. dancing, driving, skating
- help to set a *mood*, e.g. a romantic mood for a candlelit dinner for two
- enhance *concentration*, e.g. when studying, driving
- provide *comfort*, e.g. for a lonely or elderly person
- provide *pleasure*, e.g. a lover of particular types of music
- help with *religious* practice, e.g. choral music and chant may inspire worship
- help to express or experience *spirituality*, e.g. a piece composed to express an inner feeling
- support a *cause*, e.g. protest songs against war or drugs.

Whatever the reason, music can have a very powerful influence on how we feel and go about our day-to-day lives. Whether a person is composing music, playing it or just listening, its importance cannot be underestimated.

> **AQA** *Examiner's tip*
>
> Remember, if you are writing about the purpose of music, an example would help to develop your answer.

B *People go to rock concerts for pleasure*

Activities

2 a From the bullet point list above, use the italic words to put the reasons why people use music in your order of importance.

   b Compare your most and least important choices with a partner. Be prepared to explain your choices.

3 'Music is more powerful than speech.' Do you agree? Give reasons for your answer, showing that you have thought about more than one point of view.

> **Summary**
>
> You should now be able to discuss and evaluate the different reasons why people listen to music.

5.2 Different types of music

Commercial music

For writers and performers, there are two main motivations for writing and performing music – fame and fortune, or as an expression of feelings.

Some write and perform commercial music in the hope that it is going to make them rich and famous. Much of this music brings pleasure to a lot of people. Commercial music can be either popular or classical but, in order to be successful, recordings have to achieve high sales. It would be unusual for a commercial recording artist to say that their motivation was anything other than fame and making money, although some do.

Objectives

Identify different types of music.

Evaluate an example of spiritual music.

A X Factor winner Leona Lewis has found fame and fortune

Spiritual music

Writers and musicians normally compose music because they want to express the emotions or feelings they have and share them with others. They may say that their music is an expression of something spiritual, without necessarily being religious. This type of music could be, for example, a beautiful piece of classical music, a song in which the words convey a message or deeper meaning or sacred music for use in worship.

∞ links

Look back to pages 8 and 9 for a discussion about spirituality. See the Glossary at the back of this book for a definition.

See pages 100–101 for a more detailed discussion about religious music.

Activities

1   Explain reasons why some people choose to compose religious or spiritual music.

2   a   List **five** examples of:
    - spiritual music
    - religious music
    - commerical music.

    b   Which list was easiest for you to compile? Explain why.

AQA **Examiner's tip**

You could use the information about Eric Clapton as an example of a musician who found that he could express his spirituality through his music.

Eric Clapton and his song 'Tears in Heaven'

Eric Clapton became a successful rock musician in the 1960s as guitarist and occasional lead singer in bands such as The Yardbirds and Cream. Since then, he has featured with several other groups and musicians before becoming a solo artist. In 1991, his four-year-old son, Conor, fell to his death from a 53rd floor window in a tragic accident. During the following nine months, Clapton gave up performing and, to help him overcome his grief, he started to write a song that he called 'Tears in Heaven'. He later asked Will Jennings, a friend and songwriter he admired, to finish the song for him. It has become one of Eric Clapton's best known songs.

Try to lsten to 'Tears in Heaven' by Eric Clapton. Lyrics can be found by searching on the interent.

Intensely personal, and written to fulfil a spiritual need, the song reached number two on the American 'Billboard' chart and won Clapton many awards including three 'Grammys' – one for Song of the Year in 1993. In 2004, he stopped playing the song (together with 'My Father's Eyes' – a song about his father who he never met and who died in 1985). He explained this unusual move by saying that he no longer felt the personal loss and found it difficult to connect with the personal feelings he once had. He acknowledged that his life had moved on and become different.

B   *Eric Clapton*

Discussion activity

With a partner, spend five minutes discussing the quotation from Eric Clapton. What do you think he was trying to say? Record your findings.

Research activity

Listen to 'Tears in Heaven' by Eric Clapton. Lyrics can be found by searching the title of the song on the internet.

Activities

3   'No one should make music just to be famous and make money.' Do you agree? Give reasons for your answer, showing that you have thought about more than one point of view.

4   Try to write eight lines of lyrics for a song that has a spiritual meaning. See if a partner can explain the feelings in the song.

Summary

You should now be able to identify different types of music and evaluate one example of spiritual music.

5.3 Religious music

What is religious music?

Many pieces of music are inspired by religious faith and worship. Such music is produced to express the deepest feelings about religious faith and how it affects feelings about life.

How and why is religious music produced?

It is hard to tell what influence God had on how a particular piece of religious music was produced. Some composers and lyricists say that they felt inspired by God, received a revelation from him or produced the music because of their devotion to him; others do not. However, the beauty of the music often makes listeners think that it must have been influenced by God. This applies, for example, to the ancient hymns and poetry in the Old Testament and Hindu scriptures, some of which have been set to music and are still used in worship. 'The Lord is my Shepherd', Psalm 23 in the Bible, is believed to have been written by King David and is still used widely in Judaism and Christianity.

Inspiration

A composer or lyricist might be inspired to compose music because of the talent that God has given them or by a desire to share their feelings with others. They might also be inspired by teachings, events or nature, all of which could be thought of as involving God.

Revelation

Some believe that God uses lyricists and composers to reveal truths about himself by speaking through them – the words and music they write and compose are revelations from God. These truths are then passed on to a wider audience through the music or lyrics.

Devotion

Religious music is usually written to express deep spiritual feelings, often of the composer's devotion to God, and to help others share in those feelings and express their own devotion to God.

Religious music, such as hymns designed to praise God, can be used to inspire worship. Gentler music may be used to create a special atmosphere for quiet contemplation and prayer in a place of worship.

Objectives

Understand the term 'religious music'.

Understand how religious music is produced.

Explore two examples of popular religious music.

∞ links

See pages 104–105 to learn how and why various types of music are used in different religions.

∞ links

Look back to pages 10–11 to remind yourself of what is meant by inspiration, revelation and devotion.

Activities

1. Do you think writers of religious music are inspired by God? Explain your opinion.
2. a What do you think the phrase: 'The Lord is my Shepherd' (Psalm 23) means?
   b What is the writer trying to say?
3. Why do you think some religious music is written to be played on an organ?

A Some religious music is written for the organ

■ Reaching a wider audience

Some religious music, while enjoyed by believers, also appeals to a wider audience. Non-believers may also enjoy the music with or without getting any special meaning from the music or the words. However, non-believers may therefore become familiar with some religious music designed to inspire worship and feelings of spirituality or to teach deep religious truths.

Case study

'Swing Low Sweet Chariot'

This American negro spiritual is a well-known expression of spirituality, associated with Christianity. It was written in the mid-19th century as a spiritual reflection on death and heaven against the background of slavery. In the 1960s, the American Civil Rights Movement adopted it in their campaigning and the folk revival made it even more popular.

In 1988, it was sung by the crowd at an England international rugby match and has subsequently been adopted by the England rugby team. It has been recorded by several different artists, as well as the England Rugby World Cup squad.

Case study

'Abide with Me'

This is another piece of music written to express religious feelings that has been adopted by sport. Since 1927, 'Abide with Me' has become a much-loved feature of the football FA Cup final. However, it was originally written as a prayer asking God to be present throughout trials of life and death. Henry Lyte wrote the words in 1847, completing them three weeks before his death. The hymn was sung at the weddings of King George VI and Queen Elizabeth II, and is still often used at Christian funerals (including that of Mother Teresa of Calcutta in 1997) and in acts of worship.

Extension activity

1 **a** Listen to the whole of 'Abide with Me' or find and read the lyrics. What do you think Lyte was trying to express?

  b Do you think the music adds to the meaning of the words?

B *Religious music is often sung before major sporting events*

Discussion activity ■■■

In a small group, discuss whether musical expressions of spirituality should be used by a sporting crowd. Record your findings.

'Abide with Me'

“ *Abide with me; fast falls the eventide;*

The darkness deepens; Lord with me abide.

When other helpers fail and comforts flee,

Help of the helpless, O abide with me. ”

Activity

4 What do you think is the meaning of the first verse of 'Abide with Me'?

AQA Examiner's tip

Remember, you do not have to use these examples in your examination. If you know of any others, you can use them instead.

Summary

You should now be able to discuss religious music and how and why it is produced. You should also be able to give at least one example of religious music.

The composer

George Frederic Handel (1685–1759), the composer of 'Zadok the Priest', was born in Germany. However, he lived most of his life in England, becoming a naturalised British citizen in 1727. He is acknowledged as one of the greatest composers of church music. The epic oratorio 'The Messiah', which contains the 'Hallelujah Chorus' is one of the best known. He also wrote non-religious pieces such as the orchestral works 'The Water Music' and 'Music for the Royal Fireworks'.

One of Handel's first commissions after becoming British was to compose the four anthems to be played at the coronation of George II. One of these was 'Zadok the Priest', which has been sung at the coronation of every British monarch since including that of Elizabeth II.

Objectives

Investigate 'Zadok the Priest' as an example of Christian choral music.

Evaluate 'Zadok the Priest' as a way of expressing spirituality.

B Sheet music for the 'Hallelujah Chorus'

A The coronation of Queen Elizabeth II

Inspiration

Handel chose the biblical account of the coronation of King Solomon as his inspiration for 'Zadok the Priest'. You can find the story in 1 Kings 1:38–40. We do not know what inspired Handel in composing the music or what led him to choose this story, although there is the obvious link to another coronation. He may have been inspired by God. He may have read the story or known of it from a reference to it at an earlier coronation in 1685. Both Zadok and Nathan the prophet were loyal to King David and happy to obey his command to crown his son Solomon, rather than another son Adonijah who had already proclaimed himself king. Handel's words are adapted from the Bible's text, but follow it quite closely:

Research activity 🔍

Using the internet, listen to some of Handel's work, including 'Zadok the Priest'.

> ## 'Zadok the Priest'
>
> 66 *Zadok, the Priest and Nathan, the Prophet anointed Solomon King.*
>
> *And all the people rejoiced, and said:*
>
> *'God save The King, long live The King, may The King live for ever!*
>
> *Amen, Hallelujah!'* 99

'Zadok the Priest' is still sung during the anointing of each new monarch. The Archbishop of Canterbury anoints new kings and queens in Westminster Abbey by placing special consecrated oil on their hands, chest and head. This most sacred part of the service comes after the new monarch has made their vows in front of the people and God, and repeated the Nicene Creed (statement of Christian belief).

The simple words make it quite clear that God is actively involved in the coronation of the new king or queen, reflecting many people's belief that he or she is chosen by God and his or her status as the head of the Church of England. As well as the words, Handel's dramatic music inspires people with a sense of the importance of the occasion, and God's role in it, for the Christian Church and for the British monarchy. The anthem may also inspire believers to express their own spirituality by praising God on such an important occasion.

As with many other great classical works, 'Zadok the Priest' is recognised as being an inspiring piece of music to many people. It has been used in films, advertising and television. Most memorably, an adaptation of it was written to introduce worldwide television coverage of European Champions League football. It is also regularly requested on classical music radio stations and has become a popular anthem in many wedding services.

Activity

1　a　Copy the words of 'Zadok the Priest'.

　　b　Close your eyes and listen to 'Zadok the Priest'. How does the music make you feel? Why do you think it inspires some people?

　　c　Why do you think 'Zadok the Priest' has been played at every British coronation since 1727? Try to think of more than one reason.

　　d　What statement does the combination of Handel's words and music make? Explain your opinion.

　　e　'"Zadok the Priest" allowed Handel to express his spirituality through his music.' Do you agree? Give reasons for your answer, showing that you have thought about more than one point of view.

AQA   *Examiner's tip*

'Zadok the Priest' is a good example of religious music to use in the examination. You can of course find other good examples of music that express spirituality.

Summary

You should now be able to discuss an example of music as an expression of spirituality.

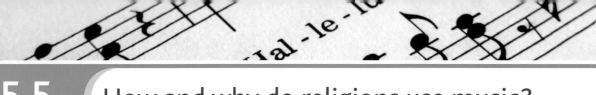

Religions' use of music

Music is more important in some religions than in others, and is used for a variety of reasons in public worship. Some religious music is also very effective for creating an appropriate mood for private worship.

Buddhism

Chanting and acoustic music played on such instruments as flutes, drums, keyboards, gongs, cymbals and hand bells are used by Buddhists. The clear-sounding melodies are designed to help Buddhists to increase awareness and communicate with the higher spiritual states of mind. Music provides a relaxing experience, often reflecting the sounds of the natural world in order to purify the mind and bring listeners in line with the Dharma (teachings of the Buddha).

Christianity

Music can be used to assist worshippers in prayer and contemplation. It is also used to praise God through singing **hymns** and in the ritual chanting and singing of prayers in religious services. Hymns, many written a long time ago, unite the whole congregation of worshippers in restating their beliefs and praising God. Some hymns include words of **scripture** put to music or paraphrases of scripture. In most Roman Catholic and Anglican churches, the words of worship have been modernised from the 16th-century form to make them easier to understand.

Hinduism

There are two main forms of music. Bhajans are devotional songs often expressing love for the Divine or any number of gods. They should be sung with devotion or love in either private or public worship or at any other time a person chooses. The musical accompaniment is on traditional Indian instruments including small drums, bamboo flutes and stringed instruments. Kirtan is call and response chanting, which involves a musician or singer singing a phrase or sentence repeated or answered by all the worshippers. Public worship also includes singing hymns and songs accompanied by dancing and instruments, and chanting hymns or mantras accompanied by a harmonium, drums and hand cymbals.

Islam

Music is not allowed in the mosque and is not necessary to worship. There is great debate about whether it is allowed at all, including in day-to-day living. It is not allowed if it highlights or encourages sinful acts. Some believe that singing is permitted, but that musical instruments are not. Strict Muslims interpret various sentences in the Qur'an and Hadith as stating that singing and listening to songs and the use of musical instruments is haram (not permitted). Others believe that as Islam provides a way of life that caters for genuine human instincts including the enjoyment of music, it should be permitted. They also point out that Muhammad allowed music at weddings and listened to girls singing.

Objectives

Understand how and why music is used in worship.

Evaluate the place of music in worship.

Key terms

Hymn: religious song.

Scripture: the sacred writings of a religion.

A   *The harmonium used in Hindu or Sikh music*

B   *The tabla drums used in Hindu or Sikh music*

Judaism

Jews have been using music in worship and for pleasure for around 3,000 years. Much of the music used in the synagogue is unaccompanied, although the organ is increasingly being used. Synagogue prayer is led in song by the cantor (chazzan) and other religious songs are often sung by the congregation as reminders of the scriptures or laws. Jews also have a strong music tradition with folk and popular songs featuring in religious and other celebrations.

Sikhism

The music played by Sikhs is similar to Hindu music and uses the same types of instruments. The shabad (devotional songs) and kirtan used in worship are taken from the Guru Granth Sahib, the Sikh scripture. They are led and accompanied by ragis, who usually play tabla (two small drums), harmonium and a stringed instrument or cymbals. In the gurdwara, the ragis sit on the right-hand side of the Guru Granth Sahib as it rests on the palki.

C   *The pungi, used by Indian snake charmers, is thought to be one way of communicating with the gods*

Summary

You should now be able to discuss how and why music is used and its place in public and private worship.

Religious music for believers and non-believers

For centuries, believers have used religious music specifically to help them feel closer to God, learn more about him and worship him. Religious music has also been written to help create an atmosphere for worship or to assist with contemplation or meditation. It is this music that some non-believers also find useful, perhaps to set the mood for their own personal reflection and meditation. Music, therefore, has an impact on believers and non-believers.

Mood music

One of the recent growth areas has been in sales of recorded music designed to enhance a person's mood. Thus, music loosely connected with the meditative religions, like Buddhism, such as chanting mantras and 'peace music', has become popular among a wide range of people. It may be used to create an atmosphere and feeling of relaxation, to calm people down or to assist thought or meditation. The recorded sounds of nature such as running water, the wind blowing through the trees or birdsong are also popular for much the same reason.

This type of music is often termed 'new age music'. The new age movement is a spiritual nature movement, which has become more popular since the 1970s. It combines spirituality, alternative and complementary medicine, environmentalism and selected religious practices from the East and West. It rejects organised religion in favour of an individual spiritual approach, and often uses music to help promote spirituality.

In a similar way, Christian Gregorian chant has become popular, with several chart successes for 'artists' such as the Benedictine Monks of the Abbey of Santo Domingo Silos. Many people buy this type of music for its soothing and relaxing quality rather than for devotional reasons, and this is how it tends to be marketed. However, some people believe it has an impact on their own spirituality.

Cultural 'folk' music

The 1990s saw an increase in the sales and popularity of 'world music'. This includes music with its roots in religion, such as Jewish folk Klezmer from Eastern Europe. This distinctive Jewish music is rooted in Jewish culture and helps to reinforce Jewish identity and tradition. It is now also enjoyed by a new non-Jewish audience. A similar thing has happened to some of the bhajans, kirtans and shabads from Hinduism and Sikhism, which have been brought to a wider audience partly through the Bollywood film industry in Mumbai in India. People enjoy listening to these types of music regardless of their religious origins or the inspirations or motivations of the writers.

Objectives

Understand how religious music affects believers and non-believers.

Analyse and evaluate the way different people perceive religious music.

AQA   Examiner's tip

If asked about the impact of religious music on people, it would be helpful to refer to different types of music.

A   *Meditation using music*

Beliefs and teachings

Music is the pulse of Jewish spirituality – song charts the biorhythms of the Jewish soul.

Chief Rabbi Sir Jonathan Sacks

Sacred choral music

B A church choir

⚭**links**

Look back to pages 102–103 for information about 'Zadok the Priest'.

Sacred choral music has been popular with lovers of classical music for centuries. In addition to the enjoyment factor, it is popular with audiences because of the effect it has on the spirit. Judaism values choral music and 20th-century Jewish composers Paul Ben-Haim and Ernest Bloch, for example, have written several pieces such as 'The Vision of a Prophet' and 'Sacred Service' respectively. Pieces such as Handel's *Messiah* and Stainer's *The Crucifixion* are often performed in church concerts for music lovers, rather than in acts of worship. Rousing hymns such as William Blake's 'Jerusalem' are used to raise the spirits of listeners, whether sung in a church or a sporting arena.

It may be that some church organists and members of church choirs and congregations attend Christian worship as much because they enjoy the music as to express their faith, especially in churches that have a reputation for the excellence of their music.

Research activity 🔍

Using the internet and/or a library, find some examples of religious music. Listen to them carefully.

Activities

1   a   Give reasons why people listen to religious music.

   b   Which reason do you think is the strongest? Give reasons for your choice.

2   'Religious music should only be used for religious purposes.' Do you agree? Give reasons for your answer, showing that you have thought about more than one point of view.

3   Explain how listening to music can affect a person in a spiritual way.

Therefore, it is clear that music based on, or inspired by, religion enjoys a wider listening audience than just those who use it in worship. The connection to the spiritual dimension is strong, even for those who listen out of enjoyment – their spirits are lifted by the music they are enjoying and they are provided with an opportunity to reflect or to meditate.

Summary

You should now know and understand the different uses of religious music and the impact it has on people, religious or not.

What does religious music tell us about God?

The answer depends on the religion and the type of music. Buddhist music tells us nothing about God because Buddhism does not have a belief in God. There is also no tradition of using religious music in Islam.

Christian music is often designed to praise God. The words or lyrics speak of his qualities – he is the all-powerful creator who sits in majesty, who forgives the sins of believers and offers them a place with him in heaven – to enable believers to praise and express their love for him. The beauty of the music tries to echo God's qualities, adding to the power and spirituality of worship. The fact that music is often performed in churches and cathedrals, which are elaborately designed and built to praise God, adds to the effect. Christian hymns and other religious musical works are usually based on themes from the Bible that speak of God's qualities or are based on biblical stories, which show God's power and care for his people.

Jewish, Hindu and Sikh music expresses the same sentiments as Christian music. Their spiritual simplicity is seen as a strength and assists quiet meditation and concentration. The music indicates the belief that people can access God personally through faith. Sikhs believe that music will help them to concentrate on meditating on God's name.

Religious music can also be tranquil and aid thought, prayer and meditation. This perhaps echoes the compassionate and forgiving side of God, who offers a way for believers to open up their thoughts to him and obtain inner peace.

Objectives

Explore what religious music tells us about God, belief and the composers and lyricists.

Evaluate religious music as a way of spiritual expression.

∞links

Look back to pages 104–105 to remind yourself of how and why religions use music.

A Cathedrals, and many ordinary churches, have dedicated choirs to lead the congregation in sung praise

Discussion activity

With a partner, discuss the following statement: 'Elaborate musical performances, with an orchestra and a large choir, distract rather than help people to praise God.' Do you agree? Give reasons for your answer, showing that you have thought about more than one point of view.

What does religious music tell us about belief?

We have seen how religious music helps people to understand God and his power. Religious music and words can also teach about other beliefs – hymns encourage people to love each other and act in a way that will bring them closer to God. They show the importance of loving your neighbour, for example. The music and words show that believers want to please God and thank him for what he has done for the human race. Using music assists praise, prayer and meditation, which are important elements in the Jewish and Christian instruction to 'love the Lord your God with all your heart and with all your soul and with all your strength' (Deuteronomy 6:5). This is the essence of what religion is all about, not only in Judaism and Christianity, but also in Hinduism and Sikhism. Music plays a part in helping this to happen and in reminding believers of their responsibilities.

Activity

1 'Religious music tells us little about religion.' Do you agree? Give reasons for your answer, showing that you have thought about more than one point of view.

What does religious music tell us about composers and lyricists?

Many pieces of religious music have both a composer (music) and lyricist (words). For example, the words of the psalms and hymns from the Bible, the Vedas and the Guru Granth Sahib were written many years before they were set to music. Composers wrote the tunes to enhance the meaning of the words, to help people remember the words and to enable them to join with others in the worship. For example, the words of 'The Lord is my Shepherd' were originally written as Psalm 23, but one setting to music of this poem (known as Crimond) was written by Jessie S. Irvine around 1850.

The composers and lyricists of religious music believed in the importance of what they were writing, especially of the hymns and poetry recorded in the holy books. They may have felt that their writing was inspired by God. While they probably did not expect their work to be so popular and long lasting, it was a way of expressing their deeply-held beliefs in a way that was respectful to the God they worshipped.

Beliefs and teachings

The LORD is my shepherd, I shall not be in want.
He makes me lie down in green Pastures,
he leads me beside quiet waters,
    he restores my soul.
He guides me in paths of righteousness for
    his name's sake.
Even though I walk
    through the valley of the shadow of
    death,
I will fear no evil,
    for you are with me;
your rod and your staff,
    they comfort me.
You prepare a table before me
    in the presence of my enemies.
You anoint my head with oil;
    my cup overflows.
Surely goodness and love will follow
    me
all the days of my life,
and I will dwell in the house of the
    LORD
forever.

Psalm 23
A psalm of David.

Activities

2 Why does a lot of religious music have a different composer and lyricist?
3 Explain how religious music enables a person to express their faith.

Summary

You should now be able to discuss what religious music tells us about God, belief and composers and lyricists. You should also be able to evaluate ways in which religious music expresses spirituality and faith.

5.8   Cat Stevens/Yusuf Islam – a case study

The early days

Cat Stevens was born Steven Demetre Georgiou in London in 1948. He had a natural love of art and music, and showed great talent for both. At the age of 15, he began writing his own songs and a couple of years later he had a recording contract. In 1966, he had a top 30 record called 'I Love my Dog'. His next hit 'Matthew and Son' reached number 2 and a string of live concert performances, alongside 1960s stars like the Jimi Hendrix Experience, established his place in the British music industry.

However, the pressure of concert appearances and battles with his record company, and a lifestyle including smoking cigarettes and drinking alcohol, took their toll. He was taken into hospital with tuberculosis. During his 12-month convalescence, he began to think deeply and became interested in Eastern religions, especially Buddhism.

The lyrics of his songs became more subtle and reflected a new inner strength, perhaps inspired by his newly found interest in religion. More hits followed, including 'Father and Son' and a simple version of the Christian hymn 'Morning has Broken' taken from the *Teaser and the Firecat* album released in October 1971.

During the early 1970s, Cat Stevens's interest in Buddhism grew stronger and began to be reflected in his music. The music and lyrics of songs such as 'The Boy with a Moon and a Star on his Head', finishing with the message that 'love is all', reflect his search for a spiritual home.

Objectives

Learn about the music of Cat Stevens (Yusuf Islam).

Relate his musical direction to his spiritual search.

A   *Cat Stevens*

Extension activity

Using the internet, listen to 'The Boy with a Moon and a Star on his Head'. Write a paragraph about what you think Cat Stevens is trying to say in the song. Discuss it with a partner if you wish.

Soon after, Cat Stevens was introduced to Islam. He was in a market in Morocco when he heard singing. When told it was Islamic music for God, he was moved. As he explained, he had heard of music for applause, for money, for praise, but this was music seeking no reward but from God. He felt this was a 'wonderful statement'.

Cat Stevens's quest for spiritual meaning was nearly at an end. In 1976, he almost drowned, swimming off the coast of Malibu in California. He called out to God when he realised his life was in danger. He said that straight afterwards, a large wave carried him back to shore. He then started to study a copy of the Qur'an his brother had given him. After months of soul searching, he converted to Islam in 1977, taking the Islamic name Yusuf Islam.

Yusuf Islam put his music career on hold. He devoted his life entirely to world peace, charity and education. He has founded and financed several Islamic primary and secondary schools in Britain, helped to establish Muslim Aid (an international relief organisation) and become a prominent figure working for the good of humanity. He has been given several international awards for his work for peace and his opposition to terrorism.

In 1995, Yusuf Islam made a tentative return to the music business, recording a spoken word album called *The Life of the Last Prophet* which brought Islamic poetry and culture to a wider audience. Several recordings have followed, but none have achieved the commercial success of his earlier work. However, commercial success is low down on his list of priorities. His spiritual search is over and he has found his spiritual home in Islam.

B   *Yusuf Islam*

> ### AQA   *Examiner's tip*
> If referring to Cat Stevens/Yusuf Islam in the examination, it might help to be clear about your points if you refer to him as Cat Stevens before his conversion to Islam and Yusuf Islam after his conversion.

> ### Research activity
> Using the internet and/or a library, find and listen to Cat Stevens's music from the 1960s and 1970s. Compare it with his music as Yusuf Islam from 1995 onwards.

Activities

1   Trace Cat Stevens's spiritual search until he became a Muslim.

2   Do you think Cat Stevens should have put his music career on hold when he became a Muslim? Explain your opinion.

Summary

You should now be able to discuss the music of Cat Stevens and how it demonstrates a spiritual search culminating in conversion to Islam.

Does spirituality influence music?

Some people say that although great music and lyrics, including specifically religious music, are composed and written by extremely talented people who may be expressing deep emotions, these emotions have nothing to do with God or spirituality. Others believe that spirituality does influence music. It would appear to be true in the case of Yusuf Islam. His music has reflected his spiritual search and now that he has embraced Islam, he produces simple music expressing deep faith.

As with other types of creativity (e.g. art, literature, architecture), it could be argued that all music is an expression of spirituality, but is not necessarily religious. Even though composers and lyricists usually need to earn a living from their composing, they can still express elements of spirituality through their music or words. However, it would be harder to find expressions of spirituality in music or lyrics if the composer had written them only to make money or become famous.

While it is possible to compose religious music and write religious lyrics without a faith, the existence of faith can add an extra dimension to the composition and may inspire the composer or lyricist. For believers, this extra dimension may help the music to communicate with an element of God within them, which is what they mean by spirituality.

However, it is not just God who may be responsible for inspiring people to write beautiful music and lyrics. Events and experiences can inspire people – the horror of war has inspired some emotional songs and poetry to express the feeling that war should not happen. Love and devotion can also provide inspiration to express deep feelings that may be seen as spiritual, as can the beauty of nature or the magnificence of a great building.

Objectives

Explore how spirituality can influence music and how music can influence spirituality.

Evaluate how much spirituality and music influence each other.

links

Look back to pages 110–111 to remind yourself about Yusuf Islam's music.

Discussion activity

With a partner or in small group, discuss what people mean when they say that they were inspired by God. Record your findings.

A   *Nature can provide inspiration*

Some people may believe that spirituality cannot influence music. However, whatever the listener thinks, the thoughts and motivations of the composer or lyricist should always be taken seriously.

Does music influence spirituality?

Just as music can be the product of spirituality or inspiration from God, listening to music can put people in touch with their spirituality or make them feel closer to God. For example, listening to beautiful choral music in the magnificent surroundings of a cathedral or to 'mood music' at home can do this. However, what is a spiritual experience for some is just pleasant music for others. Everybody is an individual and we all respond to things in different ways.

However, music does play an important role in inspiring spirituality in Christian, Hindu, Jewish and Sikh worship. For example, praising God is a spiritual activity encouraged by the singing of hymns, and communicating with God is helped through the use of prayers set to music.

B   *Music can help inspire spiritual feeling*

Pop idols

In February 2002, Will Young was voted the first winner of the show *Pop Idol* and he has now achieved commercial success in the music business. He became an idol, as many other musicians do, to many pop music lovers. However, the word 'idol' means a statue or image of God produced for worship. Does this mean that music artists are treated like gods? Many people do seem to idolise their favourite musicians or bands and it might be argued that, to them, the performer almost becomes a substitute for God. In listening to the music, attending concerts and collecting memorabilia, it could be said that they are, in a way, worshipping their favourite performer.

The symbolism of religious music

Religious believers think that religious music has a much deeper impact than pop music. It is symbolic in many ways and on many different levels:

- Composing elaborate and beautiful music shows that only the best is good enough for God.
- The type and quality of music used for psalms and hymns show respect to their origins in holy books or as compositions inspired by God.
- The volume and tempo of music may symbolise different types of worship. Hymns of praise are rousing, whereas hymns that express personal spiritual truths are often quieter and more reflective.
- The very fact that believers feel that it is important to praise God with music is symbolic of the respect they have for him. For them, it is an acknowledgement that God is almighty and humans are his creation put on earth to serve him and to use their talents to praise him.
- Many hymns and other pieces of religious music have existed for hundreds of years. Their continued existence symbolises centuries of belief and tradition associated with a particular religion.
- The note or tone of an instrument, perhaps a drum or bell, symbolises the presence of holiness. Hindus ring a bell once before worship to alert the deity of their presence.
- Sound seems to rise upward, which is symbolic of prayers and worship rising to God.
- Lyrics or words can be deeply symbolic to convey meaning, as shown in the Christian hymn 'Jerusalem'.

Objectives

Explore positive and negative uses of symbolism in music.

Explore the symbolism in religious music.

A *Bells are used in Hindu Temples*

Discussion activity

1 With a partner, discuss the following statement:

'The concert hall becomes the place of worship, the music symbolises the ritual and teaching and the performer is regarded as a god.' Do you agree? Give reasons for your answer, showing that you have thought about more than one point of view.

B *Pop musicians often become the idols of teenage girls*

There is some debate about what the hymn 'Jerusalem' is about. One interpretation is that it is linked to the coming of Jesus to England (there is a legend that Jesus visited Glastonbury in England with his uncle Joseph of Arimathea). In Christian thinking, Jerusalem is a symbol for heaven, which the hymn contrasts with the industrialised development of England's green and pleasant land. The hymn could be interpreted as saying that Jesus briefly created heaven on earth in England and so we should aim to recreate it, despite the problems of an industrialised country.

AQA   *Examiner's tip*

If you use 'Jerusalem' as an example in the examination, there is no need to write out all the lyrics.

Beliefs and teachings

'Jerusalem'

And did those feet in ancient time
Walk upon England's mountain green?
And was the holy Lamb of God
On England's pleasant pastures seen?
And did the countenance divine
Shine forth upon our clouded hills?
And was Jerusalem builded here
Among those dark satanic mills?

Bring me my bow of burning gold!
Bring me my arrows of desire!
Bring me my spear! O clouds, unfold!
Bring me my chariot of fire!
I will not cease from mental fight,
Nor shall my sword sleep in my hand,
Till we have built Jerusalem
In England's green and pleasant land

William Blake

C   *The lake district – heaven on earth?*

Discussion activity

2   Think of another symbolic interpretation of the hymn 'Jerusalem'. Discuss this with a partner. Record your findings.

Activities

1   Choose **three** of the ways that music can be symbolic from the bullet-point list. Explain each in more detail, giving examples if possible.

2   Are there any ideas on the list that you disagree with? What are they and why do you disagree?

Summary

You should now be able to discuss aspects of symbolism in music, and especially the symbolism in religious music.

5

Religion and music – summary

For the examination you should now be able to:

✔ discuss and evaluate why people listen to music

✔ identify different types of religious music, including hymns, mainstream music, chanting, scripture put to music

✔ explain what is meant by 'religious music'

✔ explain how religious music is produced, through inspiration, revelation and devotion

✔ discuss how and why religion uses music

✔ explain how music is used in public and private worship

✔ discuss and evaluate the impact of religious music on believers and non-believers

✔ discuss what religious music tells us about God, belief and composers/lyricists

✔ discuss the symbolic nature of music as a form of spirituality

✔ give examples of music to show an understanding of what makes them an expression of spirituality.

Sample answer

1   Write an answer to the following examination question:

'Nobody can be inspired by God to write religious music.' What do you think? Explain your opinion.   *(3 marks)*

2   Read the following sample answer:

> I disagree with this statement. You only have to listen to some religious music like 'Zadok the Priest' and the 'Hallelujah Chorus' to realise that no person could compose anything so beautiful without God's help. In addition, the ancient psalms and hymns from Judaism and Hinduism are amazingly poetic and express ideas about God that are in advance of what people thought about him when they were written. Of course God inspired them.

3   With a partner, discuss the sample answer. Do you think that there are other things that the student could have included in the answer?

4   What mark would you give this answer out of 3? (Look at the mark scheme in the Introduction on page 7 (AO2) before you attempt this.) What are the reasons for the mark you have given?

AQA Examination-style questions

1 Look at the illustration and answer the following questions.

(a) Give **two** ways in which religion uses music. *(2 marks)*

 Examiner's tip All you need to write is two words or phrases to say how religion uses music. However, because the question says '**give two ways**', a sentence for each one may be useful.

(b) Explain what religious music may tell us about God. *(3 marks)*

 Examiner's tip When you are asked to explain, make sure that you give some detail. If you refer to a specific piece of music, try to include the title.

(c) 'Religious music only interests religious people.' What do you think? Explain your opinion. *(3 marks)*

 Examiner's tip Here, you are asked to give your opinion about whether religious music only has an impact on religious people. Think about some religious music you have heard. You don't have to give an alternative point of view.

(d) Name and describe a piece of religious music you have studied. *(4 marks)*

 Examiner's tip You must name the music you are writing about. When describing it, include why it was written, what it sounds like to you and, if it has lyrics or words, what are they about.

(e) 'Music should have no part to play in religion.' Do you agree? Give reasons for your answer, showing that you have thought about more than one point of view. Refer to religious arguments in your answer. *(6 marks)*

 Examiner's tip You need to think carefully of reasons why some people think music should have no part in religion and reasons why other people think it should. Then write a short paragraph (5–7 lines) for each side. If you have time, finish with a conclusion, without repeating yourself. Write between 12–15 lines altogether.

6 Religion in contemporary society

6.1 The expression of spirituality in society

A materialistic society

A *A busy shopping street*

Objectives

Distinguish between the materialistic and the spiritual.

Identify ways in which spirituality is expressed in society.

Key terms

Community: a group within which a person lives and acts, e.g. a religious community.

OO links

Look back to pages 8–9 to remind yourself about spirituality.

OO links

Look back to pages 8–9 to read about materialism in more detail. See the Glossary at the back of this book for a definition.

In the UK, we live in a materialistic society where getting what we want and need for a comfortable life is seen as very important. Despite economic downturns from time to time, many people seem to find the money for the latest fashions or gadgets without too many problems. Of course, there are many who for various reasons do not buy these luxuries, but they tend to get overlooked in most people's desire to have whatever they want.

Some years ago, people lived without mobile phones. They had to because mobile phones had not been invented. If people were out, they had to use a public callbox if they needed to contact anybody. Nowadays, not only do most people have a mobile phone, but they change it regularly as technology advances and manufacturers and retailers tempt them with new offers. In 20 years, the mobile phone has gone from an exclusive gadget for the rich to something that is seen as a necessity for most people.

With a partner, discuss the following statement: 'There is more to life than buying more and more possessions.' Do you agree? Give reasons for your answer, showing that you have thought about more than one point of view.

Spiritual society

There are some people who do not adopt a consumerist way of thinking. For them, there are more important things than possessions. They believe that what we have on the outside will not change what we are on the inside, which is more important. Some people pursue the spiritual element in their life by living in a spiritual **community** away from the rest of society. Their focus is on expressing their spirituality through their religious observances. Others try to focus on their spirituality within normal society. They may become a priest or other religious leader, but many will express their spirituality through their own individual commitment to their faith, or by living with piety (great devotion to God through worship, prayer and mediation).

Another way that people can express their spirituality is to work with others in society in an attempt to make lives better. For example, for some, working for a charitable organisation is an expression of their spirituality. This could be a response to the religious teachings to care for others that are found in all religions or to humanist principles of helping each other because we all share a common bond of humanity. For these people, compassion for others is as important as religious ritual and equally as valid spiritually. Many believers regard their work in helping others to be part of their response to their beliefs – an outward expression of an inner faith.

This emphasis on the spiritual rather than the material can help to give a meaning and purpose to our existence and help us to interpret what happens to us. The Dalai Lama, leader of Tibetan Buddhists, sums up the difference between spiritual and material very well:

B *Helping others can be an expression of spirituality*

Activities

1 What do you think the quotation by the Dalai Lama means? You can discuss this with a partner or think about it on your own.

2 Explain the different ways people can express their spirituality in society.

3 Which of these ways do you think is best? Explain your opinion.

4 'Helping others is a duty, not an expression of spirituality.' Do you agree? Give reasons for your answer, showing that you have thought about more than one point of view.

Beliefs and teachings

Human happiness and human satisfaction must ultimately come from within oneself. It is wrong to expect some final satisfaction to come from money or from a computer.

The Dalai Lama

Summary

You should now have considered different approaches to life and be able to discuss some ways in which spirituality is expressed in society.

AQA *Examiner's tip*

If using a quotation, try to include the name of the person you are quoting.

What does membership of a faith involve?

Choosing to follow a faith

Everyone chooses whether or not to follow a faith. Some people reject the idea with little thought and others accept belief as an obvious choice, perhaps because they are brought up in a religious home. However, many people make a conscious choice to follow a faith after a great deal of thought and deliberation. Indeed, some join one faith and then change to another. For those who choose to follow a faith, faith makes two demands on them – specific religious observance, such as prayer and worship, and the application of their beliefs to everyday decisions and their way of life so as to have a positive impact on those around them and wider society.

Religious observance

All faiths require followers to worship, pray or meditate. This can take the form of visiting a place of worship on regular occasions or worshipping at home. Worship may follow a set pattern, as in some denominations of Christianity and Islam, or it could be more individual or improvised, as in Buddhism and Hinduism. However, many religions and denominations offer a combination of both kinds of worship depending on the purpose.

All forms of worship involve prayer or meditation as a way of contacting God or, especially in Buddhism (which does not teach that there is a God), developing mindfulness, concentration, peace and insight. Praise and learning from holy books or a religious leader also feature prominently in worship.

Objectives

Understand the demands that following a faith makes on a person.

Reflect on the effect these demands have on the life of a believer.

Discussion activity 👥

In a small group, tell each other how much thought you have given to following a religious faith. Have you made any decisions?

A *Muslims praying*

Religious observance can include other spiritual disciplines as well as worship. For example, Muslims have a duty to fast and to undertake a pilgrimage to show their faith. In all other faiths, pilgrimage is an optional element that some believers find helpful. Jews are expected to obey laws or kashrut, which govern the types of food they eat, and to observe Shabbat rituals associated with their Friday evening meal.

A way of life

Faith makes other demands on believers. Apart from those who become monks or nuns, as in Christianity and Buddhism, or devote themselves to study or spiritual development, believers should have a positive impact on society. Every religion encourages believers to follow the teachings of their faith when making decisions about their own behaviour and lifestyle. This can be extended to actively helping the poor and needy in their own society or in other parts of the world. Some people choose to devote their lives to development work or the relief of poverty overseas. They may even become a missionary, not only caring for the physical needs, but also the spiritual needs, of the people they encounter.

AQA Examiner's tip

Remember, not all believers follow their faith as strictly as others. You could make this point in an answer about religious practice.

Research activity

Find out more about the spiritual disciplines in the religion(s) you are studying.

Case study

Nursing missionary in Chad, Africa

Alison has been working as a missionary for 12 years. After her husband died, she decided she wanted to do something different with her life. After a period of soul searching, including asking God what he wanted her to do, she felt she had an answer. She decided that she should use her nursing skills by working for a missionary organisation.

> *I was asked to go to Chad to work in a health centre with Julie, a trained midwife, and one of the local doctors. Our job is to look after the people from surrounding villages and immunise them against disease. We also advise them about their general health and about contraception – one of the problems they face is overpopulation. We make no secret of the fact that we are Christians. Many people we treat are keen to find out about our faith and some have joined their local church as a result. For the first time in my life, I feel that I am doing what God wants me to do.*
>
> Alison

B Chad is in central Africa

Activities

1. Explain the demands that faith makes on a follower.
2. Should missionaries keep their religious faith a secret? Explain your opinion.
3. 'Religion makes too many demands on followers.' Do you agree? Give reasons for your answer, showing that you have thought about more than one point of view.

Summary

You should now be able to identify some of the demands religious faith makes on a believer, and evaluate the effect they have on a believer's life.

Religious communities

Living in a monastery

Some people believe that they can express their spirituality best by living in a **monastic** community as monks (male) or nuns (female). In Buddhism, the Sangha (order of monks) is highly valued. Indeed Theravadan Buddhists believe that being a monk is essential for achieving enlightenment. Most young Buddhist boys (and some girls) spend some of their teenage years living as a monk in a monastery as part of their education and spiritual development.

The Christians who become monks feel a 'calling from God' at some stage of their life and decide to follow it. During the training, which can last up to nine years, their 'calling' is tested and some decide the life of a monk is not for them. Others complete the training and spend the rest of their life as a monk. Monks believe they develop their spirituality by prayer, worship and work, either just within their own monastic community or within the wider community.

Living in a faith commune

Some people choose to live in a **faith commune**, run on the principles of a particular religion. In Israel, over 100,000 people live in communes called kibbutzim (communal settlements). Although some are not religious, other kibbutzim follow the Orthodox Jewish tradition and its religious teachings. Any devout Jew can be accepted into an Orthodox kibbutz as long as they are prepared to conform to the high level of Jewish observance required. This will involve such things as attending synagogue, observing festivals and keeping laws such as Shabbat and kashrut (food laws).

Objectives

Investigate what monastic, commune and community membership of a religion means.

Evaluate these ways of living as an expression of spirituality.

Key terms

Monastic: relating to the lifestyle of monks and nuns.

Faith commune: community of people who live their lives through the teachings of a faith; often people visit these for set periods of time rather than live in them permanently.

Religious community: a group of people from the same religion.

Denomination: one of the worldwide Christian traditions such as Roman Catholic, Methodist, Anglican, etc.

∞ links

See pages 124–125 for more information on a Christian community.

A *Theravadan Buddhist monks*

The first kibbutz was established around 100 years ago by young Jewish pioneers, mainly from Eastern Europe, who were seeking to make a new life for themselves in Israel, their homeland. There are now around 270 kibbutzim in Israel, ranging in size from 300 to 4000 adult members. They are democratic rural communities dedicated to mutual aid and based on the principle of joint ownership of property, following the idea of 'from each according to his ability, to each according to his needs' – a phrase popularised by Karl Marx to explain his communist philosophy.

Most kibbutzim are laid out to a similar plan. There is a residential area with a communal dining hall, and a library, medical clinic, laundry, synagogue and leisure facilities like a swimming pool and bar. The children (who see their parents for just a few hours a day) live in a communal house with playgrounds. The farm animals and fields are kept close by.

B   *Eilot kibbutz, Southern Israel*

Living with faith in everyday life

Most believers from all religions live alongside everybody else in society. It is likely that they will choose to belong to a **religious community** based in a place of worship. They may feel that belonging to a religious community helps them to contribute a religious element to society and to influence it for the good of other people. Most will be lay members; a few will become religious leaders. Believers of some faiths also have to decide which **denomination** to belong to. For example, Christians might choose between being a Roman Catholic or a member of the Church of England, whereas Jews might choose Orthodox or Reformed Judaism.

Individual religious communities are usually centred around a particular place of worship, and often have a role in the wider society as well as in the religious community. For example, they teach children about the faith and offer opportunities for social interaction; they may also provide a place for believers and non believers to meet, and help disadvantaged people. Every Sikh gurdwara has a langar (free canteen) which can be used by anybody. This gives believers a chance to make friends with other believers, to welcome visitors and also ask for the advice of the granthi (priest) or other community leaders.

Activities

1 Make a list of the differences between a monastery and a kibbutz.

2 What do you think the phrase "from each according to his ability, to each according to his needs" means?

Extension activity

How would you feel about being brought up in a kibbutz rather than at home? Give reasons for your answer.

AQA *Examiner's tip*

If using a technical term in your exam, you do not need to provide an explanation in brackets.

Activities

3 Explain why most people choose to live in the community rather than in a monastery or commune.

4 Which of these three ways of living do you think helps a person to best develop and express their spirituality? Think of reasons for each one before making a decision.

Summary

You should now be able to discuss the different religious communities that people may choose to live in, and evaluate these choices as an expression of spirituality.

Belmont Abbey, Hereford – a case study

A Benedictine monastery

Belmont Abbey in Hereford is an example of a Christian monastic community. Founded in 1859, it is home to 40 monks from the Benedictine order, most of whom are ordained priests in the Roman Catholic Church. The monks follow the rules laid down by St Benedict, who was born in Italy in 480 CE. After becoming a hermit, and following the strict 'Rule of the Master' Benedict moved to Monte Cassino, between Rome and Naples, in Italy and wrote his own 'rule' – 'The Rule of St Benedict', which is a little easier to live by than the 'Rule of the Master'. It consists of 73 short chapters and is now usually accompanied by a commentary to give advice on keeping it. The Rule is still kept by all Benedictine monks.

Objectives

Find out about a specific monastic community.

Understand how monks express their spirituality.

Activity

1   Spend 10 minutes making a list of rules you follow in your day-to-day life.

A *Abbey Church at Belmont Abbey*

The Abbey Church at Belmont, which also serves as a parish church, is dedicated to St Michael. It has a side chapel dedicated to St Benedict, who is pictured behind the altar holding a copy of his Rule. To demonstrate the importance of this chapel, it houses a reliquary, a special container holding what is believed to be a fragment of the wood of the cross on which Jesus was crucified. The Abbey Church is also used by anyone in the local community who chooses to worship there.

A monk's life

The Rule of St Benedict requires monks to worship seven times every day. At Belmont, this has been reduced to five times by combining some of the shorter services. The day starts with a service called Morning Office at 6.30am, followed by a community mass at 8.00am at which anybody from the local community is welcome, whether or not they are a monk. After breakfast at 8.30am, the monks work at a variety of jobs either within the abbey or out in the wider community. For example, those who have been ordained might work as a priest in a local church. Midday Prayer is at 12.45pm, followed by a formal lunch at 1.00pm. Lunch is eaten in the refectory in complete silence, apart from one monk who is appointed to read to the others. A vocabulary of sign language has been developed to ask for things. After more work in the afternoon, the fourth service, Vespers, starts at 6.00pm and the final one, Compline, follows supper at 8.00pm. The abbey is silent from 9.45pm until the next morning. There are also two periods of half an hour set apart each day for personal reading and prayer.

This routine helps the monks to develop their spirituality by focusing their lives on God. The fact that they have all their needs, such as food and accommodation, provided for (including a payment of £50 per month for essentials) means they have no financial worries, which also helps them to focus on their spiritual advancement.

Activity

2   a   Explain how living at Belmont Abbey helps the monks to develop their spirituality.

    b   Do you think this is a good way for a believer to live? Explain your opinion.

Discussion activity

Discuss with a partner whether you agree that it is easier to develop spirituality when you have no financial worries. Record your findings.

Thoughtful reading of the Bible (*Lectio Divina*)

One way of furthering spirituality, laid down in the Rule of St Benedict, is by *Lectio Divina*, or the thoughtful reading of the Bible. The aim is not to 'get through the Bible', but for the Bible to 'get through to you'. Therefore, a short passage is read slowly and re-read several times while questioning in depth what each word or phrase is trying to say. This allows a prayerful 'conversation' with God so that he can speak to the reader through the scripture. This can then be a topic of deep contemplation or reflection, which may sometimes be aided by using a piece of religious art related to the reading.

Examiner's tip

You could refer to thoughtful reading of the Bible in the religion and literature topic if you are asked about the use of religious literature.

Activity

3   'It is better to let the Bible get through to you than for you to get through the Bible.' Do you agree? Give reasons for your answer, showing that you have thought about more than one point of view.

B   *Thoughtful reading of the Bible at Belmont Abbey*

Extension activity

What piece of writing, religious or not, would you choose to provide an opportunity for spiritual reflection? Explain your reasons.

Summary

You should now be able to discuss a specific monastic community and explain how monks express their spirituality.

6.5 Religious symbols

Religious clothing

Often people can be identified as a member of a particular faith by the way they look. For example, they may wear special clothes. Muslims are expected to dress modestly. Many choose loose flowing garments such as a galabiyya for men and a jilbab and headscarf or a burqa for women, which are less likely to attract unwanted attention from members of the opposite sex. Some Muslim women also choose to wear a veil that covers their face apart from their eyes. Islamic dress has been a matter of debate in recent times: many claim it is religious and therefore compulsory, others claim it is cultural and therefore a matter of choice.

Although lay Buddhists can choose how they dress, they are also expected to dress modestly. On the other hand, monks are required as a duty to wear a robe that is usually orange, red or yellow. Most Christian monks and nuns also wear special clothing, as do priests when leading worship. Priests and ministers in most Christian denominations often wear a white clerical collar, sometimes called a dog collar, as a symbol of their role.

Research activity

1   Using the internet and/or a library, find out more about the vestments (clothing) that Roman Catholic or Church of England priests wear in worship. What is the significance of the colours they wear at different times of the year?

Activities

1   Do you think religious faith should influence or dictate what a person wears? Explain your opinion.
2   What do you think 'dressing modestly' means?

A *A Muslim family*

Religious symbols

Each religion has at least one **symbol** that people may wear, often on a chain around the neck to show they belong to a particular faith. However, non-believers may decide to wear a religious symbol for other reasons. Not everybody who wears the Star of David around their neck is Jewish and the same can be said about the cross, the symbol of Christianity. The ancient Hindu swastika symbol was adopted by the Nazi Party in Germany in the 20th century, despite their political philosophy being far removed from Hinduism. For Hindus, it means good luck and prosperity.

In the 1990s, purity or chastity rings became popular amongst some Christian girls, especially in the USA, who were making a statement that they intended to remain virgins until they married. In Britain in 2007, Judge Michael Supperstone QC ruled that a purity ring is not an essential part of the Christian faith and that the ring is not a religious artefact. He was making a ruling on a case brought by a 16-year-old girl who was challenging her school's decision that she could not wear her ring in school.

However, some symbols are recognised as essential elements in a faith. Male and female Sikhs who have chosen to become Khalsa Sikhs are required to wear the Five Ks, although for reasons of practicality not all Khalsa Sikhs wear them all.

The Five Ks are:

- Kesh – uncut hair, which for the sake of tidiness is kept in a turban

- kangha – a small wooden comb, often worn in the turban, which reminds Sikhs that even though their hair is long, it must be tidy. It is symbolic of the need to keep their life in order by 'combing away' impure thoughts

- kara – a plain steel or iron bracelet, which is worn on the right wrist as a reminder that God is eternal and, like the bangle, has no beginning or end

- kachera – baggy undershorts as a reminder of modesty, but also because historically they allowed easy movement in battle

- kirpan – a ceremonial sword as a reminder that there is a spiritual battle to be fought, defending the weak and oppressed, and upholding truth. Most Sikhs carry a very small kirpan for reasons of legality and practicality.

B   *A Khalsa Sikh*

AQA   *Examiner's tip*

If you cannot remember the Punjabi words for the Five Ks, the English translations are acceptable.

Activities

3   Pick out all the religious symbols mentioned here. Categorise them into two columns: one for those that are compulsory (duty), the other for those that are worn through choice.

4   Why do you think people with no religious faith choose to wear religious symbols?

5   'If a Sikh is allowed to wear a kara in school, a Christian should be allowed to wear a purity ring.' Do you agree? Give reasons for your answer, showing that you have thought about more than one point of view.

Research activity 🔍

2   Find out about the special clothing and symbols connected with the religion(s) you are studying.

Summary

You should now be able to identify the different types of religious symbols, discuss why people wear special clothes and symbols of their religion, and evaluate their use.

Nadia Eweida – a case study

Problems with wearing religious symbols

Although most people are happy for others to wear religious symbols if they choose, there are occasions when they are not allowed. In France, it is illegal for any school pupil in a government-run school to wear a visible symbol from any religion. A number of French pupils have been permanently excluded for breaking the ban, mainly Muslim girls who have refused to remove their headscarves (hijabs).

Discussion activity

With a partner, in a small group or as a whole class, discuss the following statement: 'School pupils should be allowed to wear religious symbols in school.' Do you agree? Give reasons for your answer, showing that you have thought about more than one point of view.

In Britain, there is no such law, although there have been isolated cases of pupils being excluded from school for wearing a kara, purity ring or hijab. Some of these cases have been subject to legal action.

A British Airways found itself at the centre of a national controversy in 2006 – about the right to wear religious symbols

Objectives

Analyse the case of a person not allowed to wear a religious symbol.

Evaluate the rights and wrongs of the case.

∞ links

Look back to pages 126–127 to remind yourself about religious clothing and symbols.

AQA Examiner's tip

If referring to a case you know of where a pupil has been disciplined by a school for wearing religious clothing or symbols, you do not need to name the pupil or the school.

Nadia Eweida and British Airways

In October 2006, there was a much publicised case of Nadia Eweida, a Christian working at a British Airways check-in desk at Heathrow airport. She was suspended from her job for refusing to remove a small cross she was wearing around her neck.

Her case raised important questions about the right to wear a religious symbol whilst wearing a work uniform. She was asked to hide the small silver cross under her uniform as others did. She refused. Her argument was that, as a Christian, she should be allowed to wear an expression of her faith openly. She compared her treatment with Sikhs being allowed to wear turbans and Muslim women being allowed to wear the hijab. British Airways argued that they made a distinction, allowing turbans and the hijab because they cannot be easily covered up, but not allowing jewellery around the neck because it can be covered up.

The response of most religious people towards Nadia was supportive.

B   *Nadia Eweida*

- The Archbishops of York and Canterbury were highly critical of British Airways and even threatened to sell the £10.25m worth of shares the Church had invested in the airline.

- The Pope's aides in charge of relations with other churches and Christian leaders from the USA and Africa all denounced the ban.

- Inayat Bunglawala from the Muslim Council of Britain pointed out that the cross is not offensive to Muslims and that Nadia should be allowed to wear it.

- Various prominent British politicians were highly critical of British Airways and suggested that people should boycott the airline.

On 25 November 2006, Willie Walsh, Chief Executive of British Airways announced a rethink on their policy. On 19 January 2007, the airline announced that small religious symbols would be permitted to be on show if worn either on a lapel pin or on a neck chain. However, in January 2008, Nadia Eweida lost her case for compensation in an employment tribunal, alleging religious discrimination.

Activities

1   a   Why did Nadia Eweida refuse to remove her cross from public view?

    b   Do you think she was right to do so? Explain your opinion.

2   Should British Airways have changed their policy? Explain your opinion.

3   'Nadia Eweida did not suffer from religious discrimination.' What do you think? Explain your opinion.

Summary

You should now be able to discuss the case of a person who fought for the right to wear a religious symbol and evaluate the rights and wrongs of the case.

Acts of worship

Worship in different religions

All religions offer their followers the opportunity to worship with others on a regular basis. While there are differences in what happens between different faiths, and even between different denominations within the same faith, there are also many similarities. **Acts of worship** are an important expression of spirituality both for the individual and for the religious community.

Buddhism

Most Buddhist worship consists of meditation, focused on developing mindfulness, concentration, peace and insight. Offerings of flowers, light or incense are made to the rupa (image of the Buddha) before the worshipper kneels or stands before the image. The leader of worship, possibly a monk, may repeat the three refuges and the five precepts before some mantras are said, followed by a period of silent meditation. Before the worship ends, the leader may give some form of teaching, perhaps based on one of the holy books.

A *A rupa with offerings of flowers*

Christianity

Christian worship varies widely according to denomination. Liturgical worship, in the Roman Catholic or Orthodox Churches or the Church of England, follows a set pattern as laid out in a missal or prayer book. It includes such activities as singing hymns, saying prayers, reading from holy books, hearing a sermon and taking part in the distribution of bread and wine to represent (or become) the body and blood of Jesus.

Non-liturgical worship does not follow a set pattern, although hymns, prayers, readings and a sermon are important elements.

Objectives

Understand what happens at an act of worship.

Reflect on similarities and differences between different acts of worship.

Key terms

Act of worship: a ritual which is followed to show devotion to God, or as part of a faith.

links

Look back to pages 120–121 to remind yourself about what it means to be a faith member.

AQA **Examiner's tip**

Remember that you may refer to one or more than one religion or denomination in this part of the examination.

Hinduism

Hindu worship takes place either at home or in a mandir (temple). The daily duties require Hindus to practise yoga and meditation, and to worship and give reverence to the deity. At home, offerings to the deities are made and mantras are said. A similar thing happens in the mandir. At congregational worship, the pandit (priest) presents offerings and recites prayers. Bhajans (hymns) are sung and an offering of fire is made to the deities by placing a lighted candle in front of one of them. Arti is then shared by passing around a tray of five lighted candles. Worshippers put their hands over the flames and then wipe their hands over their heads as a symbol of receiving God's power.

Islam

Followers are required to pray five times daily either in the mosque or at home. In the mosque, the imam leads set prayers before worshippers make their own personal prayers. It is important that Muslims are able to concentrate on their prayers, so they try to remove all distractions and pray in a plainly decorated prayer hall. On Friday lunchtimes, the imam or another respected Muslim preaches a sermon.

Judaism

Believers are encouraged to worship in the synagogue on Shabbat (a day of rest and worship starting on Friday evenings at sunset). This act of worship takes place every Saturday morning, although many orthodox synagogues offer the opportunity to worship twice daily. Despite differences between Ultra Orthodox, Orthodox and Reformed worship, the structure is similar. The main activities are the procession of and readings from the scrolls, the sermon, and prayers and hymns either in Hebrew or English, or a combination of both.

Sikhism

There is no special holy day, but congregational worship in Britain tends to be on a Sunday. Services last several hours, but Sikhs can come and go as they please. The main focus is the Guru Granth Sahib. Readings are made and hymns are sung. Worshippers are encouraged to meditate on what they hear being read. When the service is finished, all worshippers are invited to share a meal in the langar (gurdwara dining hall).

links

Look back to pages 104–105 to remind yourself about bhajans.

B   *Offerings are used in Hindu worship*

C   *A Sikh gurdwara welcomes anybody to eat in the langar*

Activities

1. Briefly write about the main features of worship in the religion(s) you are studying.
2. Do you think worship in a special building is better than worship at home? Explain your opinion.
3. 'Worship is very similar whatever religion it is from.' Do you agree? Give reasons for your answer, showing that you have thought about more than one point of view.

Extension activity

'Acts of worship are a total waste of time.' Do you agree? Give reasons for your answer, showing that you have thought about more than one point of view.

Summary

You should now be able to discuss what happens in worship in different religions and evaluate the similarities and differences.

6.8 How does worship affect individual people?

How does worship affect individual worshippers?

The fact that all religions offer followers the opportunity to worship, and that various activities feature in all religions, seem to indicate that worship is a valuable activity that many people want to take part in.

Personal worship

This tends to focus on prayer, meditation or praise. Many people feel the desire or need to talk to God in a personal way, perhaps to confess, to thank him for his influence in their lives or to ask for guidance. They may feel that this helps them to find out about and live the sort of life God wants them to live. There is nobody else involved, just the individual and their God.

In theistic religions, meditation and prayer involve thinking deeply about an issue, problem or a teaching as a way to open a channel for two-way communication with God. Meditation enables non-theistic Buddhists to connect with their inner being.

Individual prayer and meditation can have a calming effect and this can bring peace and relaxation to the lives of believers. However, many who do not follow organised religion also practise meditation and yoga to relieve stress and to focus the mind on the spiritual rather than the physical aspects of life.

Objectives

Understand the effects and benefits that worship can have on individual believers, communities of worshippers and the wider society.

A *Personal worship*

Discussion activity

With a partner or in a small group, discuss the following statement: 'If more people meditated, the world would be a more peaceful place.' Do you agree? Give reasons for your answer, showing that you have thought about more than one point of view.

AQA **Examiner's tip**

Make sure that you clearly state whether you are writing about individual or community worship.

Community worship

Worship with fellow believers can have a similar effect, but can also give worshippers a great sense of community. It often takes place in an inspiring building, where praising God seems to be the natural thing to do. Singing hymns of praise with others and with musical accompaniment is a way of showing devotion and thanksgiving to God. Community worship also gives believers the opportunity to learn more about their faith from their holy book, from the person leading the worship or from each other. Worshippers may feel more secure in their faith knowing that others share it and offer support to each other. Social interaction with other believers is especially valuable if a person spends most of their day-to-day life with people who do not share their faith.

How does worship affect society?

Many people are non-believers and do not attend acts of worship; some believers might also say that they do not feel the need to attend acts of worship regularly. However, others would say that we all have a spiritual side and that we all feel the need to pray or worship at some point during our lives. This often happens in times of great need. For example, during the Second World War, churches in Britain were full every Sunday as people prayed for the safety of members of their family or friends and for the souls of those who had died. Many also believed that God was on their side and would step in to help them win the war. Once the war was over, attendance at church fell. People sometimes find themselves involved in prayer in times of personal crisis.

Places of worship are open to everybody, regardless of whether or not they have a faith. Priests, and sometimes other worshippers, will give their time to help anybody who needs it.

Many people from minority religious or ethnic groups find the fact that the place of worship is a centre of the community comforting. They appreciate the help that it provides as they try to live in a society that is sometimes hostile to them. They may choose not to worship there, but still derive great benefit from talking to people who do and from attending community events or activities.

B *Their religion has helped Jewish communities survive centuries of persecution*

C *Worshipping together helps give Muslims a strong sense of community*

Activities

1. Explain how individual worship can help a believer.
2. What does community worship add to individual worship for the believer?
3. 'How a person worships has nothing to do with anybody else.' What do you think? Explain your opinion.

Extension activity

Evaluate whether a place of worship should be used as a focal point for the community, regardless of whether or not the individuals attending are religious.

Summary

You should now be able to discuss the reasons why people worship and the effect their worship has on them as individuals and on the community at large.

The impact of religion

Salt and light

In Matthew's Gospel, Jesus is quoted as saying:

Beliefs and teachings

You are the salt of the earth. But if the salt loses its saltiness, how can it be made salty again? … You are the light of the world. A city on a hill cannot be hidden. Neither do people light a lamp and put it under a bowl. Instead they put it on its stand, and it gives light to everyone in the house. In the same way, let your light shine before men, that they may see your good deeds and praise your Father in heaven.

Matthew 5:13–16

There are different interpretations of these verses, but they can be seen as teaching Christians that they should add flavour to society and preserve good things in the way that salt does. Their faith should be shown in their actions for others, so that their faith reflects well on God rather than being hidden away. Followers of other religions have a similar duty to help others and demonstrate their faith.

Discussion activity

With a partner or in a small group, discuss the following statement: 'Faith should have an effect on the individual, which in turn affects society through the good actions it produces.' Do you agree? Give reasons for your answer, showing that you have thought about more than one point of view.

Religion's impact on the individual

For many people, following a religion is a response to their spiritual search for meaning. Their faith provides the answers to questions such as 'Why am I here?' and 'What happens when I die?'

Even though religion throws up difficult questions, believers are happy that they have a faith to help them work out the answers, possibly through prayer, meditation, reading holy books or consulting religious leaders. Religion gives their life a purpose and meaning through following the teachings and having confidence that God will have mercy and forgive them if they go wrong.

Objectives

Understand the impact religion has on individual believers and society at large.

Evaluate the rights and wrongs of religion's impact on society.

A *'Let your light shine before men'*

B

Individual Christians, drawing spiritual strength from their religion, may decide that serving God is part of their everyday life and work as they face the challenges of trying to help and support others. Confidence that God is involved in their life may inspire some believers to take risks in their desire to help others. Becoming a missionary overseas, for example, is at the expense of personal comfort and carries greater risk than a comfortable life at home. Working with those in extreme poverty in Britain, as the Salvation Army does, also carries risks and demands a strong conviction that it is what God wants them to do.

∞ links

Look back to pages 120–121 for a missionary's case study.

Extension activity

Several overseas missionaries have been murdered by members of the communities they were trying to help. Do you think overseas missionaries should be banned for their own safety? Explain your opinion.

Research activity 🔍

Find out more about the Salvation Army at www.salvationarmy.org.uk.

◼ Religion's impact on society

Religion can impact on society in various ways. Voluntary and missionary work are ways of helping vulnerable members of society, something that believers are encouraged to do. Lay Buddhists are expected to provide food for monks to earn good karma. Religious charities such as Islamic Relief and Christian Aid provide emergency aid and fund long-term projects in many places around the world. There are also hundreds of charities, funded by all religions and staffed by believers, working with the underprivileged in Britain.

British history and culture is influenced strongly by religion. The British monarch is the Head of the Church of England and two archbishops and 24 bishops have seats in the House of Lords – the highest decision-making body in the country. In addition to Christianity, different faiths also add their own flavour to society and to our ever-evolving culture.

C   *Different faiths add flavour to society*

Activities

1   Explain how a person's religion can affect their own life.
2   Is it fair to expect religious people to help the poor? Explain your opinion.
3   'The Christian Church should have no part in the running of the country.' What do you think? Explain your opinion.

Summary

You should now be able to discuss how religion affects individuals and society, and evaluate the rights and wrongs of how it affects society.

The reaction of other people

While many people believe that everybody has a spiritual side and the capacity to develop it in their day-to-day life, some people show little interest in recognising this. Many ignore the expressions of faith displayed by religious people. However, some may show hostility towards religion and ridicule those who practise their faith. A few people, who may be tolerant of a particular religion, are actively hostile to followers of other religions. This irrational dislike of whole groups of people and individuals within them is called prejudice. This becomes discrimination when the dislike is demonstrated by denying people of other faiths and cultures the equal opportunities they are entitled to. On occasions, this has resulted in a deliberate decision not to employ someone, provide accommodation for them or has even resulted in violence, with gangs picking on religious or racial minorities.

Objectives

Investigate difficulties arising from expressing spirituality.

Compare reactions to historical and modern expressions of spirituality.

A *Some groups can isolate someone who is seen as different*

Activities

1. a Note down reactions you have observed, both positive and negative, to religious people.
   b How do you feel about those reactions?
2. How do you respond to people who display their faith in their everyday life?

Case study

Sir Cliff Richard is a very well-known British singer and entertainer. He has had top 10 records in every decade from the 1950s to 2000s. During his career, Cliff has sold more than 250 million records, with around 120 singles and albums making the top 20. Concert tours sell out within hours of tickets going on sale.

In 1964, Cliff became a practising Christian and, after much thought and prayer, decided to continue his music career, but to avoid becoming part of the sex, drugs and alcohol culture that many successful bands and artists at that time were involved in. While most of his songs have no Christian content, he has recorded several compilations of Christian songs, three of which have reached number one in the Christmas singles charts.

However, despite his massive success, he is still ridiculed by some people because of his faith and the way he lives his life.

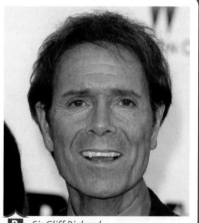

B *Sir Cliff Richard*

Discussion activity

With a partner, discuss whether Sir Cliff Richard should be ridiculed for his faith or admired for his achievements. Is there a different response – other than ridicule and admiration – that people may have towards him? Record your findings.

Historical displays of spirituality

It is interesting to note that historical displays of spirituality in such fields as art, architecture and music are widely admired. One of the most beautiful European cities is Venice. Every year between 15 and 20 million tourists visit the city to marvel at the breathtaking churches, including St Mark's Basilica, and religious art by some of the world's greatest artists, including Tintoretto and Titian.

Research activity

Using the internet and/or a library, find out about some of the religious art that can be seen in Venice.

C *St Mark's Basilica, Venice*

More up-to-date displays of spirituality in these fields do not attract such attention. The Shri Swaminarayan Mandir in London was opened in 1995. It is the largest traditionally built mandir in the western hemisphere. The marble and limestone blocks from which it is built were carved by approximately 1,500 craftsmen. The *Readers Digest* has described it as the eighth wonder of the world, but it does not receive the same amount of attention as older, more established places of worship. Modern religious art and music tends not to be as highly regarded as that produced centuries ago either. Perhaps in time, modern expressions of spirituality will become more admired than they are now.

Activities

3   Why do you think historical displays of spirituality appear to be admired more than modern ones?

4   Do you think that modern expressions of spirituality will be better regarded in the future than they are now? Explain your opinion.

AQA *Examiner's tip*

If you are asked to explain anything, always try to include an example to support your explanation, even if you are not specifically asked to.

Summary

You should now be able to discuss reactions to expressions of spirituality and be able to give your own opinions about them.

6

Religion in contemporary society – summary

In the examination you should now be able to:

✓ identify and evaluate the ways spirituality is expressed in society

✓ understand the demands that following a faith makes and the effects of those demands on the individual

✓ give examples of different types of religious community and understand what membership involves

✓ understand and evaluate why people wear special clothes and religious symbols, and the problems they may face in doing so

✓ understand and evaluate the importance and spiritual benefits of attendance at acts of worship

✓ understand the effects of worship on the individual, communities of worshippers and society

✓ understand the impact religion has on individual believers and society

✓ understand and evaluate the difficulties arising from expressions of spirituality.

Sample answer

1. Write an answer to the following examination question:

   'Nobody should be allowed to wear a religious symbol.'
   Do you agree? Give reasons for your answer, showing that you have thought about more than one point of view. Refer to religious arguments in your answer. *(6 marks)*

2. Read the following sample answer:

   > I agree that nobody should be allowed to wear religious symbols because all it does is cause trouble. Take the lady at the airport who wore a cross. How much trouble has she caused and for what? It is also not safe to have Sikhs wandering around with swords because their religion says they have to carry one. They are completely uncool anyway so they should all be banned.

3. With a partner, discuss the sample answer. Do you think that there are other things that the student could have included in the answer?

4. What mark would you give this answer out of 6? (Look at the mark scheme in the Introduction on page 7 (AO2) before you attempt this.) What are the reasons for the mark you have given?

AQA Examination-style questions

1 Look at the photograph and answer the following questions.

(a) Explain why some religious people choose to belong to a monastic community. *(3 marks)*

 Remember, if you are asked to explain, you need to give some detail and perhaps an example to support your answer.

(b) 'Religious people should *all* live in society like everybody else.' What do you think? Explain your opinion. *(3 marks)*

 Here, you are asked to give your opinion. However, it is important that you give reasons for your opinion because it is the evidence and reasons you give that will earn you marks.

(c) Give **two** symbols that religious people may wear. *(2 marks)*

 The word 'give' means that you can write down two symbols and you don't need to provide any detail.

(d) Explain **two** reasons why a religious person might choose to attend an act of worship. *(4 marks)*

 You only need to include two reasons, but need to develop each one in order to explain it clearly and achieve two marks for each reason.

(e) 'Worship should only be done in the home.' Do you agree? Give reasons for your answer, showing that you have thought about more than one point of view. Refer to religious arguments in your answer. *(6 marks)*

 You need to think about why some people think that worship should only be done in the home and why others think it should be done elsewhere instead of, or in addition to, the home. You should then write both sides of the discussion, including religious content, in 12–15 lines.

Glossary

A

Act of worship: a ritual which is followed to show devotion to God, or as part of faith.

Agnostic: a person who believes it is not possible to be sure whether God exists or not.

Architecture: buildings, statues.

Art: range of visual images, made by people, e.g. paintings, calligraphy, icons.

Atheist: a person who believes that there is no God.

B

Blasphemy: talk or behaviour that insults God or the gods.

British Board of Film Classification (BBFC): official body which classifies films in the UK according to their suitability to be shown to different age groups.

Broadcasting Standards Commission: official body which deals with complaints from the public in the UK, especially about television and radio programmes.

C

Calligraphy: stylised writing, often associated with Islam, which turns words into beautiful pictures.

Categorisation of films: the way in which films are given certificates to ensure that only people for whom the film is suitable get to see it.

Censorship: when a group (often the State) do not let the public have access to certain things, often relating to the media.

Ceremony: a ritualistic service.

Charity: giving to the needy; An organisation that does not work for profit and which usually works to help others.

Comforter : Christians believe that the Holy Spirit is with

them helping them, aiding them through life.

Commitment: (within marriage) vows or promises to be faithful to one's partner for life.

Community: a group within which a person lives and acts, e.g. a religious community.

Compassion: a feeling of pity that makes one want to help.

Conscience: the inner feeling you are doing right or wrong.

Conversion: when a person becomes a member of a faith, often following a dramatic change of heart.

Corporate worship: worship performed together as a congregation.

Covenant: a binding agreement made in the presence of God.

D

Denomination: one of the worldwide Christian traditions such as Roman Catholic, Methodist, Anglican, etc.

Devotion: dedicated to something, for example to one's religion.

Discipline: having self control.

Discrimination: to act against someone on the basis of sex, race, religion, etc. This is usually a negative action.

E

Edifice: large, imposing building, often dedicated to some person/event.

Eternal life: everlasting life after death.

F

Faith commune: community of people who live their lives through the teachings of a faith; often people visit these for set periods of time rather than live in them permanently.

Faith community: the group who worship together; this term can apply to any faith.

Forgiveness: showing grace and mercy and pardoning someone for what they have done wrong.

Free will: having the ability to choose or determine one's own actions.

G

General revelation: God making himself known through ordinary, common human experiences.

Graffiti: street art, whereby words and images are sprayed onto walls.

H

Hymn: religious song.

I

Icon: painting or mosaic of Jesus or the saints. They are more than simply aids to prayer, as they are seen as being filled with the spirit of the person shown.

Individual commitment: the extent of a person's personal devotion and involvement in their faith.

Independent Television Commission (ITC): the body which controlled commercial television companies in the UK, until 29 December 2003. It was replaced by Ofcom.

Indoctrination: teaching someone to accept without question certain beliefs, ideas and stories.

Initiation: being entered formally into a religion.

Inspiration: something which stimulates or has a beneficial, uplifting effect on the mood and senses.

Internet: an information-carrying medium that can be accessed from computers and some other modern inventions.

L

Literature: range of writings, e.g. stories, scripture, diaries and poems.

M

Materialism: belief in the importance of personal possessions.

Meditation: contemplation on religious matters.

Media: the organisations which convey information to the public, especially television and the printed press.

Monastic: relating to the lifestyle of monks and nuns.

Monotheism: belief in one God.

Monument: often large statue which is set up in commemoration of a person(s) or event.

O

Ofcom: the body which controls commercial television companies in the UK, introduce on 29 December 2003. It replaced the ITC.

P

Pastoral support: help received from religious leaders in personal matters.

Personal God: God is an individual or person with whom people are able to have a relationship or feel close to.

Piety: extremely holy or religious.

Prayer: words of praise, thanks or sorrow, etc. offered to God or to the gods.

Prejudice: unfairly judging someone before the facts are known.

R

Reincarnation: being reborn again in another form.

Religious authorities: the various groups that lead the world faiths.

Religious community: a group of people from the same religion.

Religious traditions: either the principal world faiths or the major Christian traditions (denominations).

Revelation: that God reveals himself: through special or general revelation.

S

Sacred texts: writings which are believed to originate from God or a god.

Sanctity of life: life is sacred because it is God-given.

Satellite broadcasting: those TV channels that are sent via satellite, especially those on the Sky network.

Scripture: the sacred writings of a religion.

Sculpture: a work of art which has been made from solid materials and is three-dimensional.

Special revelation: God making himself known through direct personal experience or an unusual specific event.

Spirituality: a sense of something which is not material of temporal, usually to do with religion.

Symbol: representing something through an image; many religions have symbols to represent the religion, or to represent beliefs within the religion.

Symbolism: when an image or action stands for something else.

T

Tradition: something that has been done for a very long time and is therefore thought to be true; Long established beliefs or customs.

Transcendent: God is beyond and outside life on Earth and the universe.

Terrestrial television: the standard TV channels that are available to all people in the UK: BBC1, BBC2, ITV1, Channel 4 and 5 (where available).

W

Watershed: the point after which television programmes are allowed to show 'adult' content: currently set at 9.00 p.m.

Website: a place on the World Wide Web devoted to a particular issue or subject.

Witness: to act or speak out on behalf of your faith (beliefs).

World wide web: the place on which websites are situated on the Internet.

Index

A

'Abide with Me' 101
acts of worship 130–131
afterlife 38
allegory 60
Angel of the North 15
Apocrypha 59
architecture 30–31
  religious 32–49
art 10
  religious 10–27
atheists *see* non-believers

B

Behzti (Bhatti) 67
belief, religious expression and
      24, 46–47, 68, 90–91, 109
believers 8
  following a faith 120–121
  and religious expression 22–23,
      27, 44, 66, 106
Belmont Abbey, Hereford
      124–125
Betjeman, Sir John 62–63
Bhatti, Gurpreet Kaur 67
Bible 58, 60, 71, 125
Blake, William 115
blasphemy 20, 23, 67, 84
Buddhism
  architecture 37, 38–39, 42, 43,
      46, 48
  art 19, 21, 24
  clothing 126
  literature 56, 58, 59, 60, 64
  monastic communities 122
  music 104, 106, 108
  worship 120, 130

C

calligraphy 14, 18, 20
categorisation of films 86
Cathy Come Home (BBC play) 52
censorship 67, 84–87
Christianity
  architecture 36, 38, 39, 40–41,
      43, 47, 48
  art 12–13, 16–17, 18, 21, 22
  communities 122, 123,
      124–125
  literature 56, 58, 59, 60,
      60–61, 62–63, 64, 65

  and the media 77, 81, 84, 87,
      88
  music 104, 106, 107, 108, 109
  use of symbols 26, 126, 127,
      129
  worship 130
Chronicles of Narnia (Lewis) 60
Clapton, Eric 99
clothing 126
community 118, 119, 122–125,
      132
composers 109
Coventry Cathedral 40–41
creation stories 70, 71
cross 26, 40, 129

D

Dasm Granth 56
Dawkins, Richard 92
denominations 122, 123
devotion 10, 11, 18, 35, 40, 57,
      100
Dhamma 59
'Diary of a Church Mouse'
      (Betjeman) 62–63
Dickens, Charles 52
Dome of the Rock, Jerusalem
      34–35
Drama in the Air (Myers) 55

E

edifices 38
Eweida, Nadia 129

F

faith communes 122
faith, following a 120–121
fiction 60
films 86–87, 93
'folk' music 106

G

Galileo 67
God, religious expression and 24,
      46, 68, 90, 108
Gormley, Antony 15
graffiti 14, 19, 23
gravestones 38
graveyards 38–39

gurdwara 34, 36, 49, 84, 123
Guru Granth Sahib 59, 65, 84

H

Hadith 59
Handel, George F. 102–103
Harrer, Heinrich 56
hermits 42
Hinduism
  architecture 39, 43, 48, 137
  art 12, 19, 21
  literature 58, 59, 60, 64, 65, 70
  music 104, 106, 108, 109
  symbolism 12, 126
  worship 84, 131
holy books 14, 18, 56, 58–59, 65,
      66, 71
hymns 104, 113, 115

I

icons 12–13, 19, 22
indoctrination 83
inspiration 10
  and religious expression 11, 16,
      34, 40, 56–57, 62, 100, 102
internet 87, 89, 93
Islam
  architecture 34–35, 38, 39, 43,
      49
  art 18, 20, 24
  clothing 126
  literature 58, 59, 61, 64, 65, 66
  and the media 77, 81, 82
  music 104–105, 111
  worship 131
Islam, Yusuf 111

J

Jalal al-Din Muhammad Rumi 61
Jerry Springer – The Opera 77, 84
'Jerusalem' (Blake) 115
Judaism
  architecture 38, 49
  art 13, 18, 20–21, 24
  communities 122–123
  literature 58, 59, 65
  music 105, 106, 107, 108, 109
  worship 131

K

kibbutzim 122–123

L

Lewis, C.S. 60
Life of Brian 87
literature 52–53, 54
   religious 54–71
'The Lord is my Shepherd' 100,
   109
lyricists 109

M

magazines 80–81, 83, 89
Mahabharata 60, 65
mandir 39, 48, 137
materialism 8, 118
media 74–93
meditation 120, 132
Milton, John 60
monastic lifestyle **122**, 124–125
monuments 38, 39
mood music 106
mosques 20, 49
Muhammad, images of 23, 82
Munshi, Hammaad 87
music 96–99
   religious 100–115
Muslims *see* Islam
Myers, L. M. 55

N

new age movement 106
newspapers 80–83, 89
non-believers and religious
   expression 23, 27, 45,
   66–67, 106

O

Oberammergau passion plays 57

P

paintings 13, 16–17, 19
places of worship 36–37, 40–43,
   48–49, 133
poetry 53, 57, 60–61
pop idols 114
prayer 19, 120, 132

private worship 21, 42–43,
   64–65, 132
producers, media 91
public worship 20–21, 36–37,
   40–41, 64, 132
purity rings 127

Q

Qur'an 18, 20, 58, 65, 66

R

religion, impact of 134–135
religious communities 122–123
*Resurrection in Cookham
      Churchyard* (Spencer)
   16–17
revelation 10
   and religious expression 11, 34,
   40, 56, 63, 100
Richard, Sir Cliff 136
Rushdie, Salman 67

S

sacred choral music 107
Satanic Verses (Rushdie) 67
satellite broadcasting 76, 88
scripture 104
sculpture 15, 19
Shiva 12
shrines 37, 43
shruti 58
Sikhism
   architecture 34, 36, 49
   art 19, 21
   langar 123
   literature 56, 59, 61, 64, 65, 71
   music 105, 106, 108, 109
   religious symbols 127
   worship 84, 131
Singh, Jaswinder 61
smriti 59
society and religion 133, 135
Spence, Sir Basil 40
Spencer, Sir Stanley 16–17
spirituality 8–9
   and architecture 31, 33
   and literature 53, 54

and the media 92–93
and music 98–99, 112–113
reactions to expressing
   136–137
in society 118–119
through art 10–11
stained glass 13, 18
statues 38–39
Stevens, Cat 110–111
stupa 37, 42, 48
The Sun 75, 80
'Swing Low Sweet Chariot' 101
symbolism 12, **126–129**
   in architecture 38–39, 41,
   48–49
   in art 12, 17, 26
   in literature 63, 70–71
   in music 114–115
synagogues 20, 36, 38, 49

T

Talmud 59
'Tears in Heaven' (Clapton) 99
television 76–79, 85, 88
Tenakh 58
terrestrial television 76
Tripitaka 58

V

Vicar of Dibley 78–79

W

Western (Wailing) Wall, Jerusalem
   35, 37
worship 120
   different religions' 130–131
   and individuals 132–133
   places of 36–37, 40–43, 48–49
   use of art in 20–21
   use of literature 64–65
writers 69

Z

'Zadok the Priest' (Handel)
   102–103